Jenny Wilson

NONE OF THEM KNEW WHY I WAS CRYING

Series Editor: Rony Robinson

Hodder & Stoughton

LONDON SYDNEY AUCKLAND TORONTO

ISBN 0 340 50854 X

First published 1989

Typeset by Litho Link Limited, Leighton, Welshpool, Powys, Wales.
Printed in Great Britain for the educational publishing division of Hodder and Stoughton Ltd, Mill Road, Dunton Green, Sevenoaks, Kent by Richard Clay Ltd, Bungay, Suffolk.

Contents

Apple Blossom Afternoon

Dave Sheasby

Cast

TANNOY

TED

INDIAN JANE

BACK-POCKET DAVE

BIG TALL WESLEY

FORMBOOK POVEY

MERSEY BILLY

In betting shop.

TANNOY: At Cheltenham, it's overcast. The going is good to soft. Non-runner in the 2.30, number 4, 'Lopside'. Jockey change in the three o'clock, number 16, 'Pypewipe', will be ridden by J. Blacker.

Fade.

TED: They were all looking at me. Their faces turned and fixed. Like in a photograph. The tannoy was telling us the dogs were going into the traps at Monmore. Marie was looking at me from behind the counter, peering over the top of her specs. And the others, Indian Jane, Back-pocket Dave, Big Tall Wesley, Mersey Billy and Formbook Povey, all looking at me. I could feel the tears on my cheeks and the pink slip of paper in my hands. I was fifty-five on that day. It was a Saturday in November and the clock on the wall said twelve minutes past four. And all this took place under the sign of Ladbrokes.

TANNOY *fades up under last.*

TANNOY: And they're going down the far side of the course and 'Pennysave' takes them along. He's closely followed by 'My Mackintosh'; some two lengths behind these is 'Crème de la Crème'. Coming to the next. This is the one before the water . . .

TED: A Saturday between the Mackeson and the Hennesey, when the form is begining to work out just that bit and you can feel the winter really taking a hold. Mum was always on about clean house, clean heart, but I make excuses to myself. Anyway, Saturday afternoons was always a bit of time off. 'Enjoy yourself, Teddy, but be careful.' I always was too, with the money side. Mum knew that. Not that I ever have that much on. So I never win much either. I reckon there's not many who do. Some people say that's why we do it but I think that's rubbish. I mean, who wants to lose? Mr Know-All Skeffington at work, I've heard *him* say that. Never been in a betting shop in his life but reckons to be an expert on human nature. Awful man. Still only half-past eleven. I leave the pussies some lunch, greedy lot, and set off. I've bags of time so I call at Wilcott for some ciggies and take it easy down to the shop. Get there early. There's always the dogs to pass the time.

Fade.

TANNOY: At Hackney, they bet 3–1, trap 4; 4–1, trap 5; 5–1, trap 1; 6–1 trap 2.

JANE: On the dot. The man himself. Morning, Edward.

TED: Jane.

JANE: Nippy out there.

TED: On the cold side, certainly.

JANE: 'Perry Mason' is out again. Second, second, second.

TED: I saw.

JANE: Today's his day. I've got him in my double. Better be his day.

TED: Last race at Haydock, isn't it?

JANE: Right.

TED: Long time to wait then.

JANE: I'm all right today. Our Deirdre's got a neighbour in. I'm having one off. Well, fair's fair. Saturday afternoon. Got to have a bit of time to yourself, eh? Isn't that what you always used to say.

TED: Did I?

JANE: You're looking a bit washed out. Taking care of yourself these days . . . you know . . . on your own?

TED: I'm doing okay.

JANE: Er . . . you don't happen to have a spare . . . er.

TED: Fag? Sure.

JANE: Ta. My saviour. 'Perry Mason'. It'll win today.

TED: *(narration)* Indian Jane. I have these names for the regulars. Just a little thing with me. I used to tell mum. She loved hearing about it, especially when she got badly at the end and never went out at all. One of the regulars is Jane. The bit about Deirdre's very sad. She'll be eighteen now; the only child. Wheelchair job. Terrible business. She got knocked down in the school yard when she was ten. A delivery van reversing. It was in the local paper. Crisps and sweets, the van. She's never walked since. Then the mister walked out and that left Jane to cope on her own. She gave up her job, the lot, to look after Deirdre full time. It hasn't been easy. I know that. Caring for someone. I call her Indian Jane because she's very free with her rouge. A few of the lads in here make fun and reckon she's 'mutton-dressed-as' but I admire her. She makes an effort when she goes out. She tries. Even to Ladbrokes on Saturday afternoons, she looks nice. There is no neighbour. She leaves Deirdre to fend on her own a few hours. I don't blame her for that. I think she deserves a little break.

TANNOY: Later betting, Hackney. They bet 2–1, trap 4. At Hackney, they're going into the traps.

JANE: Never touch dogs. Can't fathom it.

TED: You only need to pick one from six.

JANE: This form guide here. 'Trap 2, 'Sally Rose', plenty of speed if she can get smart out of the box. Must watch her inside.' I mean, what kind of help is that?

TANNOY: Off, Hackney. At 12.21.

JANE: My Uncle Stan owned a dog. It never won a race. A lovely name though. 'Starry Starry Tess'.

TED: A bitch, then.

JANE: What?

TED: It'd have been a bitch then. Tess.

Enter DAVE.

DAVE: Now then, you sinners.

JANE: Morning, David.

DAVE: Who's doing what, and are you sure you should be?

JANE: Touch of frost I reckon.

DAVE: It's very quiet in here. Not mourning your losses already?

JANE: It's you that's early. 'Perry Mason' is in the last race at Haydock.

DAVE: Cheltenham today. Always a nice little challenge is Cheltenham.

TED: *(narration)* Back-pocket Dave. He's a plumber. Very busy man. Always in a rush. Pressed for time, if not cash. Thing about Dave is, he wins. Not all the time, but enough. He seems to make it pay. You can't say that for many in here. Back-pocket of Dave's overalls, he's got this wad of cash. He gets tips does Dave and he's not selfish with his info. If you happen to be nearby you can click. A month ago he gave me 'Scorchlight'. It won at 7–1. I had 50p on that. Very nice too.

DAVE: I've got this central heating job on. A real swine. Can I make that boiler fire on automatic time-switch? I've come here for a break from it. Little woman's going crackers about it. I've told her I'm trying my best. Very nice lady too. Lovely eyes.

JANE: He's off.

DAVE: Not yet; be right. Not yet.

JANE: Always fancying, you.

DAVE: Me? Why didn't you tell me darling?

JANE: All mouth and no trousers . . .

She moves off.

DAVE: And how's Edward these days? Got any winners? I'll tell you what *won't* win. 'Perry Mason'.

TED: Any, er . . . bits of news?

DAVE: I did get a little nod, as a matter of fact; yesterday. Stable job. No guarantees, mind.

TED: I know that.

DAVE: First race at Cheltenham. The one on the screens now.

TED: It's a novice hurdle with thirty runners, Dave.

DAVE: Right.

TED: Half of 'em have never run. I was going to give it a miss actually.

DAVE: Like I say, It's just a nod. The price might be very affectionate. 'Bally Ferriter'. Number 30. Bottom of the shop.

TED: It's not even in the s.p. probables.*

DAVE: I shouldn't let that put you off.

*'s.p.'– starting prices; 'probables'– horses likely to run; 's.p. probables'– the odds the bookmakers will probably offer on the horses that will probably run in the race itself. The actual odds go on changing until the race actually starts, depending on how much money is put on each horse by then.

TED: Tricky race. All those unknowns.

DAVE: Listen. I've had ten nods from this lad and eight have gone in. Okay, one was disqualified after a steward's enquiry but I'm counting it because it won by four lengths going away. So, eight out of ten. That's not flat beer, Edward. Think about it. Mind you, it could be the wrong day; do a wallop. No cast iron in this game.

TED: Tempting, though.

DAVE: Please yourself. Know anything about boilers? Central heating kind?

TED: Not really, sorry.

DAVE: I just can't bear the idea of letting Mrs Lovely Eyes down. Not when she's all on her ownio – with the kiddies, mind. Still, first things first.

TED: *(narration)* And it's into the back-pocket and out, with a wad thick as a book. Now I normally just do a 20p, 30p yankee*, small bets, pay tax. Reckon on an outlay of £4 max. Just nice for a Saturday afternoon. Mum always knew I was careful with the cash side so she never had to worry. But today I'm fifty-five and I don't have a little outing in front of me tonight. For the first time. I've just realised – our little treat at the Maharajah. There's no point in going on my own. I don't want to sit in the corner like a lemon, with all those folks jabbering and eating. So I won't go out. So, looked at that way, I have spare cash . . . and it's my birthday and I've only myself to think about . . . I'll have a little roll-up bet, a little accumulator.* Why not?

*'yankee'–a four-horse bet, consisting of six doubles (two horses), four doubles (three horses) and one accumulator (four horses). If only one horse wins, the bookie takes all. If two or more win, the gambler gets some money back. If all four win, the bookmaker almost certainly has to pay out quite a lot–especially on the accumulator.

*'accumulator'–a bet on several successive races (in this case, four). All four horses have to win, both the stake and the winnings being carried forward from one race to the next.

One down, all down. It's a dream bet, really, if they all win. If it loses, well, I can always have a double later. It's my birthday.

TANNOY: At Crayford, they bet 7–1, trap 6; 2–1, trap 2; 3–1, trap 5; 5–1, trap 4; 10–1, trap 1; 10–1, trap 3. All quoted, Crayford.

Enter WESLEY.

WESLEY: Morning, my friends, how's it all shapin' up this morning?

JANE: Morning, Wesley.

WESLEY: Mornin' to you, madam.

JANE: Joys of spring, is it?

WESLEY: It's always joys of spring with Wesley.

JANE: How do you manage it?

WESLEY: Come back to the house one day and I'll show you.

JANE: Cheeky bugger. You men. In this shop. You're all the same.

WESLEY: It's you; making yourself look like a lovely lady every Saturday for Wesley. I miss you in the week, you know.

JANE: You've seen 'Perry Mason' is running again, Wesley?

WESLEY: It'll win today. We've backed it and backed it, haven't we? It can't lose today. Sir Charles Dobson's the owner and he's got to have a winner one day.

TED: *(narration)* Big Tall Wesley. Reckons to be a joiner but his back went and it's not coming back, he says, so he spends his time in here most days. Saves on the electric, he says. And he laughs but it's only half a joke. There's a few in here like that. They've got nothing and they do nothing and they need to keep warm and they like a chat. I don't think I could do that. Not all day, every day, all year round. At least I've still got my little job at Crossleys; like mum said, it keeps me out of mischief. Not that it's forever. What is these days? Skeffington's always muttering about cutbacks. He lets everyone hear just so we're all a bit afraid. I can see what Skeffo's game is, oh yes . . .

TANNOY: Opening show at Cheltenham. They go, 4–1, number 13, 'Crazyman Crazy'; 5–1, number 2, 'Knittingley'; 6–1, number 6, 'Cooper's Pet'; same price, 6–1, number 13 . . . 'Frenchman'; 8–1 bar.

Fade.

DAVE: There you go . . . not mentioned.

TED: That's what worries me, Dave.

DAVE: Take it or leave it, old love. Eight out of ten, remember. But don't blame me *if*.

TED: Right.

DAVE: I've done it anyway.

TED: *(narration)* So I take 'Bally Ferriter' as the first of my four. I need three others and I've only got five minutes. It's that kind of bet. You have to be on from the start. You choose the horses and that's it. One down, all down. It's a silly bet, really. A pools-win dream bet. Still . . .

TANNOY: Approaching the traps, Crayford. Later betting Cheltenham, they bet 7–2, number 13, 'Crazyman Crazy' . . .

Fade.

Enter POVEY.

POVEY: You've seen it, then?

JANE: Here he is. Pens down everybody. Attention.

WESLEY: Seen what?

POVEY: The three o'clock at Chepstow.

JANE: Is this a tip then?

POVEY: I'm just saying – have you seen it?

WESLEY: You're going to tell us.

POVEY: 'Karenski'. Number 16. Bottom weight.

JANE: 'Karenski'. Bottom weight, he says.

POVEY: It's gone all the way from Dorset to Wales, right? It's set to carry next to nothing, right? And who's riding?

JANE: Boy George.

POVEY: Danny Smart. Right? Claiming four pounds. There'll be a gamble on it. You watch.

JANE: What *is* he on about now?

TED: *(narration)* Barry Povey. Formbook Povey, I call him. Says he's a student. Economics, he says. He's in here a lot, I'll say that. Quite an expert. Certainly sounds like one. Very keen on form is Barry. All the details. Half the time I can't even understand him. He knows so much. And he's got all the jargon right. Student of horses – I don't know about economics.

POVEY: All right, then. You tell me why Frank Henderson's gone to such trouble to run 'Karenski' at Chepstow. I mean, see the clues and solve the mystery. If you're doing a yankee, I should make it your banker. Teddy, you do yankees.

TED: *(narration)* Yes I do but I'm not doing 'Karenski'. Instead I go for 'Pickles' and 'Bardwell Boy' – two I've followed before. They both owe me. 'Pickles' has got to come good one day soon and 'Bardwell Boy' was second at Ascot three weeks ago and was really unlucky. It was on telly, and you could see it was hampered at the second last. That was three. I needed one more for my accumulator. Then I saw it. In the last race at Cheltenham. Now I don't go on names. Mum used to. When she had a little flutter on the National or the Derby, she always went for a name. The ladies are like that, I've noticed. Indian Jane, a real case for names. They're influenced by all that sort of thing. Mind you, it can pay off. When mum was on the National that time, she picked this horse ridden by Bob Champion because she knew a lad when she was a girl called Bobby Champion. He was in her class at junior school. And this horse went and won at 11–1. I put a pound on for her. She was thrilled. 'Aldaniti'– that was it. She went and won on a name, which was more than I did. So here I am this afternoon staring at this horse called 'Apple Blossom Time' and saying to myself, don't be daft, Ted, because you don't do names. Even so . . . There was this song mum always sang when she started cleaning on a Friday afternoon. I was supposed to keep out of the way. I don't think she even knew she was doing it but it was a sort of signal that she was going to have a go at 'corners, cupboards and carpets'. Always this song and there was this horse and it was my birthday and I was thinking of mum today a lot. I don't know. It just seemed to be right even though I never go on names. Horse number four for my roll-up bet. 'Apple Blossom Time'. I put up a two-quid stake. I wrote it out and I paid tax. Total outlay, two pounds twenty pence. Daft bet, really . . .

TANNOY: At the post, Cheltenham. At Cheltenham they bet, 3–1, number 13, 'Crazyman Crazy'; 5–1, number 6, 'Cooper's Pet'.

Fade.

Enter BILLY.

BILLY: Now then. All set?

JANE: Trouble's here. Everybody say, hello.

BILLY: Ta very much. You are saying, hello, to one of the all-time great losers.

JANE: Or not saying, hello, as the case may be.

POVEY: All right, Billy? Not gone up in smoke yet?

BILLY: What have I done?

JANE: Didn't expect to see you.

BILLY: Not see me? I *live* here.

JANE: After last Saturday. You were in a right state.

BILLY: You would be. Forty-seven losers on the trot I've had. Forty-seven bets – twenty-two seconds, six thirds and the rest bloody nowhere. That can't be right. Not one winner in forty-seven bets.

WESLEY: Who gets winners? Only the Queen and the rich folk get winners. The rest of us just have to scrape.

BILLY: I've kept a note. My black book. Here. Look at this, Wesley.

JANE: Calm down. They've not even started racing yet, Billy.

BILLY: Second, third! Second, third, nowhere; second, last! Forty-seven bets. No winners. That's not natural, that.

TANNOY: Orders, Cheltenham.

BILLY: I'm doing 'Cooper's Pet' in this. It'll be second. Bet you it'll be second.

TED: *(narration)* Mersey Billy. Six foot four and half barmy. He's always like this. Always losing, always angry. Marie had to tell him off once a few weeks back. Not just the bad language. He went and jabbed his biro through the list of runners on the wall. Mind, he did say sorry afterwards. Funny, but mum always liked hearing about Billy the best.

She could never understand why he bothered to carry on with it. 'Why does he bother if he always loses', she used to ask me. I couldn't explain that to her . . . too difficult.

TANNOY: Off, Cheltenham. Off at 1.03. On the off they were betting 4–1, the field.

JANE: I've done nothing in this.

BILLY: 'Cooper's Pet' will be second. I know it.

POVEY: Novice hurdle. Thirty runners. You need brain surgery if you bet on this. Total bloody lottery. Thirty novices. Anything could win. Anyone for surgery?

JANE: He does go on, doesn't he?

WESLEY: I've done the favourite. one of Sheikh Tamrood's. He can be relied on, can Sheikh Tamrood.

POVEY: 'Crazyman Crazy'? You've actually put money on that. You must be.

WESLEY: I must be what?

TANNOY: Going out into the country for the final time at Cheltenham and it's 'Cooper's Pet' who takes them along. He's followed by 'Davos', two lengths back in second.

Fade.

TED: *(narration)* The shop's filling up now. Marie, who settles all the bets, sits at the back behind the counter, looking like a schoolteacher with those specs and her hair done up in a bun. It's all women of course, the staff.

TANNOY: Approaching the last at Cheltenham and 'Crazyman Crazy' is racing with 'Bally Ferriter'. These two have gone six lengths up on the rest. 'Cooper's Pet' is a long way back in third.

TED: Doris lives over Roebuck's butchers. She's a widow lady, and there's Miriam, whose hubby brings her every morning in the little Metro, on the dot at 10.15. It's a sort of club, really. People know each other.

TANNOY: On the run in now at Cheltenham. Two furlongs to go and 'Crazyman Crazy' and 'Bally Ferriter' are stride for stride. It's eight lengths back to 'Cooper's Pet' in third. Into the last two hundred yards now and 'Bally Ferriter' has taken a slight advantage. This one's holding on. As they go for the line it's 'Bally Ferriter' by a length now. At the line it's number 30, 'Bally Ferriter', the winner; second number 13, 'Crazyman Crazy' . . . The third horse was number 10, 'Cricket Bat'.

Fade.

DAVE: There you go, Edward. Nine out of eleven. I told you he was a good lad. See you later, old love. Must get back to my boiler lady. Those eyes . . .

TANNOY: Starting price of the winner at Cheltenham, 25–1. The favourite 'Crazyman Crazy' at 3–1 was second.

JANE: Twenty-five to one. That's a start to the proceedings.

POVEY: Told you. These races are a lottery. Leave them alone.

BILLY: Number 48. What happened to 'Cooper's Pet'? Lost in fog. Still running. Forty-eight losers. Is this a record?

POVEY: What did you do, Ted?

TED: Well – that one, actually.

JANE: You never . . .

TED: I had a tip.

JANE: Who tipped that?

TED: Dave.

POVEY: Plumber Dave? You kid?

TED: He said it had a chance.

POVEY: He might have let us all in on it.

JANE: Hark at him. You wouldn't have backed it if he'd written it in ten-foot high letters on the bloody ceiling.

POVEY: I wish he'd have said, that's all.

BILLY: Where is he anyway?

TED: On some job, he said.

BILLY: Always on some job, Dave.

JANE: No mucky talk, thank you very much.

TED: He said about a faulty boiler.

JANE: 'Bally Ferriter', 25–1. Nice one. Irish, wasn't it? Irish name anyway.

WESLEY: They have some good horses over there.

BILLY: Pity they didn't tell us about 'em in advance.

TED: I've only done it in an accumulator.

JANE: Accumulator? What's got into you?

POVEY: That was not wise, old son.

TED: No, well, I don't come in here to be wise, do I?

BILLY: I like it. I like it.

POVEY: He had a bit on himself, I suppose? Dave?

TED: I suppose he did.

BILLY: How many to go, then?

TED: What?

BILLY: In your roll-up?

TED: Er . . . three more.

BILLY: Nice start; 25–1 winner.

POVEY: See this one.

JANE: Here we go.

POVEY: 'Columbo Jumbo'. In the two o'clock at Chepstow. I mean, why have they sent it to run in a race of three miles when said horse has never, in its life, run more than two and a quarter miles, and when it last ran two and a quarter it finished pulled up? I repeat, *pulled up*! Can anyone tell me why this horse is in Wales today, running three miles against good class chasers like 'Vagabond'?

WESLEY: You ask a lot of questions, Mr Povey.

POVEY: It's 5–1 possible s.p. in my paper. Do you reckon there's something they're not telling us?

JANE: It's that university – your trouble.

POVEY: Polytechnic.

WESLEY: You think 'Columbo Jumbo' is going to win? Let me get this straight.

POVEY: I'm just asking, that's all.

WESLEY: Asking? Tell me what's gonna win, please.

BILLY: Ring him up.

POVEY: Who?

BILLY: This trainer. Illingworth. Ring him up and ask him.

POVEY: Don't talk so daft.

WESLEY: Lots of questions. But never any bleedin' answers.

TED: *(narration)* Twenty-five to one! Fifty quid! Silly man. Should've backed it to win. Still, fifty pounds; well, fifty-two, with the stake back. Might as well enjoy the moment.

POVEY: I was begged off coming here this morning.

BILLY: You what?

POVEY: A bloke came up to me in the street and asked me for 'the price of a cup of coffee, guv'.

BILLY: What did you do?

JANE: Told him about 'Columbo Jumbo'!

POVEY: He had 'Nijinsky' tattooed on the fist. Big, thick, blue letters. Back of his hand.

BILLY: A racing man, then.

JANE: How do you mean?

BILLY: Where've you been since rock'n'roll, old love? 'Nijinsky'. Bloody brilliant racehorse. On the flat. Years ago. Come on, come on . . . you *must* know.

JANE: I thought he was a dancer, Nijinsky.

BILLY: Don't be daft. Dancer? With a name like that?

JANE: You know *so* much.

WESLEY: All of it, total bloody rubbish.

TANNOY: At Haydock, they bet 2–1, number 6, 'Crispin's Day'; 3–1, number 13, 'Curley'; 5–1, number 1, 'Barley Wine'; 7–1, number 20, 'Glassily' . . .

Fade.

Enter DAVE.

DAVE: Now then. All on 'Bally Ferriter', were you?

BILLY: You might have told us.

DAVE: You never asked.

JANE: Twenty-five to one. Where do you find them, Dave?

DAVE: It was a valve. Tiny as that.

JANE: What was?

DAVE: Causing all the trouble. *The boiler.*

JANE: Have you got any more like that this afternoon?

DAVE: I wish I had. And *ever* so grateful.

POVEY: Look at this. Now this is a nice little problem.

JANE: Leave me out, Professor.

POVEY: 'Beatledrive'. In the 3.45. Top weight, right? Eleven stone, twelve pounds. Over two miles, right?

JANE: I should've done 'Bally Ferriter'. Lovely name.

POVEY: Won only once last year, and this year has only managed a crappy fifth to 'Gringo' at Worcester six weeks ago. Right? That said, why is it quoted as 3–1 favourite in the s.p. probables in the *Sporting Life.*

WESLEY: Misprint.

POVEY: Don't be daft.

TANNOY: At Haydock they bet 7–4, number 6, 'Crispin's Day'. They're going down at Haydock.

Cut to . . .

TED: *(narration)* I pass this shop sometimes in the dark at night, or on a Sunday when it's all shut up, and it reminds me of a church. A church without the people and the prayers and the singing. Lonely and silent and dark and shut up. Out of place somehow and unreal. Ladbrokes is like that. It doesn't have any point when there's no-one there.

JANE: Now then, Teddy, I can't cadge – er – another fag off you, can I?

TED: Sure.

WESLEY: Another nail in your little coffin.

JANE: You don't mind, do you?

TED: Go on.

JANE: You're a star, only I'm not smoking anymore, you see, so I can't buy any, can I?

BILLY: Not smoking?

JANE: Ta.

BILLY: Bloody marvellous.

WESLEY: Lady Waplington's got one in this next at Haydock.

POVEY: You what?

WESLEY: She's on holiday at the moment. In California. It's lovely over there this time of the year.

POVEY: How do you know all this?

WESLEY: Everybody knows about California.

POVEY: No, I meant . . . never mind.

WESLEY: She gets some winners, does Lady Waplington. She knows horses, you see. Worth following.

POVEY: What do you reckon for this next then, Billy? At Cheltenham.

WESLEY: 'Bulbrook' should walk it.

POVEY: 'Bulbrook'? Doubt if it'll get up that hill at the end of three and a half miles.

BILLY: It's done the distance.

POVEY: But not that weight. Cheltenham can tire the fittest.

BILLY: You ever been, like?

POVEY: Where?

BILLY: To Cheltenham. Know it personally, do you?

POVEY: I had a girlfriend came from Cheltenham. I never got invited back home. She got a 2.1. Business Studies. Always in the rotten library.

BILLY: I went once. Twenty years ago. Festival meeting. Gold Cup Day. I had twenty quid on 'The Laird'.

POVEY: I wasn't born.

BILLY: Course it was second. I love being on the course. There's nothing like it. The flat's best. Nicer weather. Newmarket. June meeting. Ideal, that is. Get there nice and early in some nice new clean clobber. Always take a lass. Some really smart piece with shoulder-length hair and neat little figure. I'd get this room for us at a country hotel, somewhere really smart, in the environs of the course and we'd have a clean, light breakfast and look through the papers and then set off to get to the course nice and early to watch the private jets and big limos arrive – the sheikhs and the lords and ladies, and the fat cats from the city, and the jocks like Cauthen and Eddery and Carson. Stroll on the heath, the warm sun on our backs and then stroll out into the paddock to have a look at the runners for the first race – two year olds, of course, and as they clip-clop round the ring my lass'd just nod and smile at number 7 – something called 'Perfect Dream', and I'd flip out five tens just for a starter and take a ticket on it from one of the bookmakers and I'd get 8–1, which is a nice price any day of the year. Then we watch the race from the stand, my lass holding her hat on as a little bit of breeze comes up off the rolling heathland. And we watch the knot of horses bang against the rail, flashing up the five-furlong course and then number 7 would come out of the pack, black and gold sleeves with gold cap, and it's across the line some two lengths clear and we collect a cool four hundred quid. But we've still the rest of the afternoon ahead, me and this lass, and the way it feels, it's never going to end . . . never going to end.

WESLEY: Shut that door, man; there's a big draught in here.

JANE: Anybody bung me a spare cig?

POVEY: Now this is what I call an interesting race.

TANNOY: At the post, Cheltenham. At Cheltenham, they bet 2–1, number 14, 'Chromosomes'; 3–1, number 6, 'Stag Night' ; 4–1, number 17, 'Coomber Boy'; 6–1, number 7, 'Raringtogo'; 8–1 bar.

JANE: Mine's not even in the betting.

POVEY: What's that?

JANE: 'Pickles'.

POVEY: No chance.

JANE: Says who?

POVEY: Suspect over fences. Look at this form. 'Fell.' 'Unseated rider.' 'Fell.' It's nearly a cripple.

JANE: That was last year. And watch your mouth, young fella . . .

POVEY: What have I said!

JANE: Never mind. I've said. That's all.

She goes off.

POVEY: What's up with her?

WESLEY: I'll tell you one day, man.

POVEY: Why can't you tell me now?

TED: Some other time, eh?

BILLY: 'Raringtogo' – he's got a chance in this.

POVEY: It's one-paced. Look at the form.

BILLY: Form says it's been second three times out of five. That's going close on my system.

POVEY: System?

JANE: It's a nice name, anyway.

BILLY: It'll do me.

JANE: 'Raringtogo'.

POVEY: They're all nice names. Think about it.

JANE: I'm taking 'Pickles', even so.

TANNOY: Orders, Cheltenham. They bet at Cheltenham, 7–4, number 14, 'Chromosomes'.

WESLEY: You got this race in your roll-up, Ted?

TED: Er . . . yes. I've done 'Pickles'.

JANE: It'll be 10–1, at least.

DAVE: You're always on about the price. Price is nothing to do with finding winners.

JANE: I'm not backing favourites, Dave.

DAVE: You want winners, don't you?

JANE: Can't afford favourites.

DAVE: That's daft. Winners are winners.

JANE: I can't back things at 7–4 and 15–8 and all that. Where's the return on that to 20p?

TANNOY: Orders and off, Cheltenham at 2.03.

JANE: Did you see those penguins last night on the box. Scream.

WESLEY: I don't think you should treat animals like that. Tin hats. Bloody cruel.

POVEY: Which channel was that on?

JANE: How do you mean, which channel?

TANNOY: And at Cheltenham there's been a faller at the first fence. Fallen, number 7, 'Raringtogo'.

BILLY: Fallen at the first! My card is marked! Someone is trying to get me! Friggin' torture! I paid good money for that.

POVEY: How do you mean, paid?

BILLY: I bought a system.

POVEY: Dicey.

BILLY: Advertised in the back of the *Life*. 'Win with Walt Thompson'.

POVEY: Con merchants.

BILLY: Who asked you?

JANE: How much? I've seen that ad.

BILLY: A tenner. Postage was on top.

POVEY: What did you get? A crystal ball?

BILLY: Shut it, Povey. It's a book. Gives you horses to follow.

POVEY: Who's Walt Thompson, then? I mean, what does he know?

TANNOY: A circuit to race at Cheltenham and it's 'Pickles' who's clear by some ten lengths. In second place comes 'Chromosomes' . . . 'Coomer Boy' races in third.

Fade.

BILLY: Reckons on sixty-per-cent success rate if you pick the right race with the right horse. It's all in this book. I mean, he's printed his bank account in the back. You can see what he won last year – six thou.

POVEY: Faked.

BILLY: You're getting to me, son.

POVEY: I'm just saying.

BILLY: It's a proper book. Printed out.

POVEY: Doesn't make it genuine, does it? I mean, 'Raringtogo'. Fell at the first.

BILLY: Bleedin' clever-dick students! I was backin' horses before you were on the planet.

TANNOY: One left to jump at Cheltenham and it's 'Pickles' with a ten-length advantage. This one's led from the start. In second place is 'Chromosomes' who's racing half a length up on 'Beverley Sister'. Coming to the last, and 'Pickles' is up and over safely, still some ten lengths clear. Running on strongly into third is 'Stag Night'. But on the run in it's 'Pickles' holding his lead; at the line, It's number 8, 'Pickles', the winner. Second, number 14, 'Chromosomes'.

JANE: There you go. Another little winner. We're laughing, Ted.

TED: Nice, yes.

JANE: At least 10–1.

TED: Do you think so?

JANE: Two up, two to go, eh?

POVEY: 'Pickles' should never have won that.

BILLY: Here he is. The wise man of the turf.

POVEY: How can a horse that finished twenty lengths behind 'Chromosomes' last time out come here today and beat it by ten! Can anybody tell me the answer?

JANE: Some of us were on it.

POVEY: I know *you* were on it. We *all* know you were on it. *Why*, I'm asking, did it win?

JANE: Form, lovey. It changes. Horses change. Like people.

POVEY: Disgraceful.

BILLY: You'll have a nice lot going on, Teddy.

TED: Not bad. I won't win though. Not all four.

BILLY: Two winners. It's a start. I've not had one for weeks!

TED: It won't come off – accumulators never do.

BILLY: You haven't done 'Caressing' in the three o'clock at Chepstow, have you?

TED: Why?

BILLY: 'Cos I've done it, that's all.

JANE: You'll get a winner, Billy, don't worry.

WESLEY: Try Lady Waplington's. In the three o'clock.

TED: *(narration)* This is getting serious. Five hundred and seventy-two pounds going on to 'Bardwell Boy'! Most I've ever won's seventy pounds. On a treble about eight years ago. I can't believe this. Five hundred and seventy-two quid. On one horse. 'Bardwell Boy'. I never gave it a thought. It's just one I'd done before. I'm loyal like that. Mum used to say, too loyal. A weakness, Edward. Too loyal to Mr Skeffington at work who's just a pig; too loyal to those cats who run rings round you and too loyal to me, your old mum. Yes, well, we made a good team, you and me, mum. We were all right. We looked after each other. If that's loyalty, then three cheers, says I. Five hundred and seventy quid on 'Bardwell Boy' . . . this is a real birthday afternoon, Edward my son . . . Too late to go back. It's only a two-pound bet, after all.

TANNOY: At Chepstow they bet, 13–8, number 14, 'Caressing'; 3–1, number 6, 'Skinflinter'; 4–1, number 4, 'Booklist'; same price 4–1, number 8; 'Bardwell Boy'; 7–1 bar.

POVEY: They're tipping some cash on the favourite.

BILLY: 'Caressing'? It's got to have a chance.

POVEY: One from your system, Billy? One from Walt?

WESLEY: Money doesn't win races, man.

POVEY: What does win races, Wesley?

BILLY: My grandad used to follow money. Poor old sod. Died following money. He never caught up. And he was always out of breath.

JANE: What's he on about?

BILLY: I'm being friggin' poetic.

JANE: It runs in the family, then.

BILLY: Poetry?

JANE: Betting. Your grandad.

BILLY: Every day he had the papers, pencil, form books.

WESLEY: He won a lot, did he?

BILLY: Course he didn't.

POVEY: Hasn't put you off the horses, though.

BILLY: If I'd been an airline pilot it might have, or a consultant in a hospital. I mean, I wouldn't have had the time to get to the shop, would I? But with me being a hod carrier and general labourer it hasn't made no difference. I've carried on the tradition.

JANE: Losing.

TANNOY: Later betting, Chepstow, they bet 11–8 number 14, 'Caressing' . . .

TED: *(narration)* Think of something else. Don't think of winning. Have a ciggy. It's worse than work this. When I get the summons from friend Skeffington – some bollocking or other. It's worse than waiting to see Skeffington.

TANNOY: Orders, Cheptow. Off, Chepstow 3.02.

JANE: You on, Wes?

WESLEY: No, I'm skint.

JANE: What about Mr Povey?

POVEY: I've done one.

JANE: Go on, tell us the secret.

POVEY: 'Skinflinter'. Shall I tell you why?

JANE: If you must.

BILLY: Keep it short, eh?

JANE: I've done 'Caressing'.

POVEY: Nice name.

JANE: Anyone got a spare ciggy?

TANNOY: At Chepstow they're going out onto the farside for the last time and Skinflinter takes them along. This one's some two lengths up on 'Raviolini'.

Fade.

TED: *(narration)* Two pounds accumulator. A bit more than I usually do but it is my birthday. And there's nothing much to celebrate this year. No little outing to the Maharajah with mum. I mean, it wasn't much, just a regular little do on my birthday, a little ritual. But I'm not going on my own. No way. All those couples enjoying themselves and there'll be me sat in the corner on my own. I couldn't face all that. So think of it like that. I've had a little bit of a bet today . . . a little bit of a birthday treat. 'Bardwell Boy' can't win this, anyway. Loyalty never pays, does it?

TANNOY: Turning into the straight at Chepstow and 'Caressing' still leads, with 'Booklist' now going into second. 'Bardwell Boy' is making a forward move. At the second last and 'Caressing' and 'Booklist' jump it together with 'Bardwell Boy', who's getting nearer in third. Behind these comes 'Skinflinter'. 'Cherry Riper' is not out of it. They're coming to the last. There's three in a line. 'Caressing', 'Booklist' and 'Bardwell Boy'. They jump the last together. All over it safely and on the run in now and it's 'Bardwell Boy', who has a slight lead from 'Caressing'. 'Booklist' is dropping back. They're into the last furlong and 'Bardwell Boy' still leads by half a length from 'Caressing'. It's 'Bardwell Boy' holding on, in the last hundred yards from 'Caressing'. Number 8, 'Bardwell Boy' is the winner; second, number 14 'Caressing'; the third horse was number 4, 'Booklist'.

BILLY: I'll give it another race, then I'm off.

POVEY: 'Skinflinter'. Bloody terrible. It beat 'Caressing' ten lengths at Ascot!

JANE: I must get some veg.

DAVE: I think you might be in the wrong shop.

POVEY: 'Bardwell' had some form. I'll give you that.

WESLEY: Teddy's laughing.

TED: Yes, well, that's three up.

POVEY: You never did that winner?

TED: I've backed it before, you see. I thought I'd give it another go.

DAVE: You'll have a fair old roll-up I reckon, Ted.

TED: Quite a bit.

DAVE: Yeah. More than quite a bit.

WESLEY: What's your last one, then?

TED: 'Apple Blossom Time'. Four o'clock at Cheltenham.

POVEY: It's done the distance.

TED: Has it?

POVEY: And it's got that Stewartson on it.

TED: Right, yes.

POVEY: He's riding some winners this year. Cocky sod. Saw him interviewed on TV. Welsh. Plenty to say, the Welsh.

TED: *(narration)* Marie is looking over her specs. At me. And she's smiling. She knows the score. I've got two thousand, eight hundred quid going on to 'Apple Blossom Time'. She'll have to ring her boss in Leeds. That's how it works. Really big wins she has to inform headquarters. I've seen that before. I saw her on the phone a minute since.

JANE: Why did you choose that one? Apple Blossom whatsit.

TED: Nice name . . . Here . . . Have a cig.

JANE: Ta very much. I should be getting back soon. And there's the shopping.

TED: You'll stay for 'Perry Mason'.

JANE: Should get back really. You known . . . suspense though, Ted. Your roll-up. I can't leave.

BILLY: Forty-nine losers on the trot.

DAVE: A bad run, Billy. We all have bad runs.

BILLY: This is not a bad run, it's hangman time. Skint. Total.

JANE: I need to get some veg before they close.

POVEY: This 'Apple Blossom Time' . . .

JANE: The great man speaks.

POVEY: It had some nice outings last year. Second at Sandown. Second at Ascot. In good company, too.

JANE: What price will it be?

POVEY: Fives or thereabouts. Dave?

DAVE: Fives. Yeah.

POVEY: Could be the big one, Ted.

TED: It won't win.

BILLY: Don't get like that. Wait until you'd had fifty 'won't wins'.

POVEY: 'Karakoram' will be the favourite. Three wins on the trot, that one.

TED: *(narration)* I didn't want to do my sums but I had to think about it. Two thousand eight hundred going on at 5–1 or thereabouts. With the stake back, I'd be taking away . . . I didn't want to think about it. And I'm stood there in the shop and these people around me chattering away hadn't any idea. They knew I was winning. Three up, one to go. They knew that; but they didn't know just how much. I think Dave had an idea. He'd seen Marie on the phone and he'd probably guessed they'd got a charlady's situation. It's what they call a really lucky bet like this one. Four horses all at big prices. A total one-off. Like the pools. I was shaking. Shaking! I had two cigarettes on the trot waiting for the last race. I'd been coming to this shop some fifteen years. I'm the senior citizen of Ladbrokes. Burncross Road branch. I go back before Big Wes and Indian Jane and they're old-stagers. I go back before Marie. I stood in the corner of the shop I'd been coming to for fifteen years and tried to work out how many bets I'd had and how much cash I'd lost. It is all losses in the end. And now I stood there. And I wanted to savour it, taste it. So much on one horse. It would never happen again. I know that. It had to lose and when it lost I'd have the memory. But there was no-one to share it with: win or lose. It hit me suddenly, for the first time since, you . . . since . . . since I was on my own . . . there was no-one else. I felt, suddenly, so bloody alone.

TANNOY: At Cheltenham, they bet 2–1, number 6, 'Holy Fellowship'; 3–1, number 10, 'Karakoram'; same price, 3–1, number 11, 'Havers'; 5–1, number 17, 'Ragtime Cowboy'; 6–1, number 19, 'Apple Blossom Time'.

POVEY: What do you reckon, Dave?

DAVE: 'Karakoram' will do me.

POVEY: Not so clever at the big fences though, is it? Been on the ground twice this season.

DAVE: If you feel like that, stick with Teddy here. Three up, one to go.

POVEY: 'Apple Blossom Time'? It's too young. No experience at this class.

DAVE: Always something wrong, isn't there?

POVEY: What?

DAVE: You always find a fault. How do you ever make up your mind, Povey? Tell me that?

WESLEY: Dave's doing 'Karakoram'. He knows how to pick winners that man.

JANE: He doesn't know everything, Wes.

WESLEY: Knows more than me, lovey. Lady Waplington's horse fell at the fourth.

JANE: Just 'cos they're rich doesn't mean they always win.

WESLEY: But it does, you see.

BILLY: I think I might pack it all in forever, after this – win or lose. I mean, what's the point? I've lost thirty quid in the last ten days. I can't afford it.

JANE: Go with Teddy.

BILLY: What on?

TED: 'Apple Blossom Time'.

BILLY: I fancy 'Holy Fellowship'.

JANE: Not turning religious, Billy?

BILLY: I will. If it helps find a winner, I'm a Hindu tomorrow.

TANNOY: Order and off, Cheltenham. Running, Cheltenham at 4.02.

JANE: You've done all right, Teddy.

TED: Yeah.

JANE: Are you okay?

TED: Bloody shaking. Look at me.

JANE: You've got a lot then? Going onto this?

TED: I can't believe it.

JANE: A real lot, eh?

TED: Nearly three thousand quid.

JANE: . . . You . . . never have! Really?

TED: At 6–1. I'm faint.

JANE: So am I. Now, never that much, is it?

TED: Keep it a bit to yourself though, eh? Please.

JANE: Course. Er – can I pinch one . . . ta.

TED: *(narration)* Keep it quiet? I should've known better. I could see the word going round. But it was like a dream now. I could see the people and hear the tannoy but it was all happening to someone else, out there.

TANNOY: Over at Cheltenham, 'Karakoram' is taking them along. He's some two lengths up on 'Havers'. 'Holy Fellowship' is in third.

This fades as inner voices take over.

POVEY: He stands to win . . . stands to win . . . bloody hell fire!

DAVE: Four in a row. There's no law against it. Doesn't happen very often, but still.

WESLEY: That is big money, man; big, big money.

JANE: Come on 'Apple Blossom'. Come on, for Ted's sake.

BILLY: A friggin' fortune. Retirement to Spain. Goodbye hod carrying.

JANE: He looks like death. White as a sheet.

POVEY: The horse simply has not got the necessary ackers.* Pity.

DAVE: Come on 'Apple Blossom'. Give the lad a break.

TANNOY: Three left to jump at Cheltenham. And 'Karakoram' continues to lead. 'Holy Fellowship' has moved into second, 'Havers' is dropping back.

WESLEY: Not even mentioned. God . . . not even mentioned.

JANE: It's not going to win; not now. Three *grand* down.

BILLY: Not 'Holy Fellowship'; not now – after fifty losers.

POVEY: Duff form this year. I feel sorry for him; bloody near the big one, I'll say that.

*'ackers'– speed.

TED: What a story, mum, rolling in at five o'clock. You'd never believe it. Win or lose, mum, it would be a lovely tale. You would have laughed and cried . . .

TANNOY: Approaching the second last at Cheltenham and 'Holy Fellowship' has taken it up. He's gone two lengths up on 'Ragtime Cowboy', who's moved into second. 'Apple Blossom Time' is starting a late run. Over the second last and 'Holy Fellowship' takes it safely; number 16, 'Apple Blossom Time' moves quickly through into second.

Fade quickly.

WESLEY: It's there, man; come on, horse, come on, come on.

JANE: 'Apple Blossom Time'. Lovely name.

POVEY: No extra at the finish, this one. It faded at Lingfield last year. Pity, really.

DAVE: Long run in at Cheltenham . . . anything can happen now.

BILLY: Take this winner from me. Take this winner from me.

TANNOY: Coming to the last at Cheltenham and it's still 'Holy Fellowship' by a length now from 'Apple Blossom Time' with 'Casual Baby' going into third. Over the last and 'Holy Fellowship' still a length clear of 'Apple Blossom Time'. On the run in and 'Holy Fellowship' continues to lead but he's being challenged now by 'Apple Blossom Time' on his outside. They're in the last furlong and these two are stride for stride. There's nothing in it. 'Holy Fellowship' and 'Apple Blossom Time'. 'Apple Blossom Time' and 'Holy Fellowship'. They're coming to the line, and still nothing in it. They've gone past the post together. It's a photo-finish, Cheltenham. Involved in the photograph, number 19 'Apple Blossom Time' and number 6 'Holy Fellowship'.

POVEY: 'Holy' has got it.

DAVE: Close. Very close, Very, very close.

JANE: Are you okay, Ted?

WESLEY: Photograph . . . No problem, Ted, no problem.

BILLY: I never thought I'd want a horse of mine to lose.

POVEY: Sounded like 'Holy Fellowship' has got it. From the commentary. Pity, really. Very close.

JANE: You would have to say that.

WESLEY: You still get half the winnings if it's a dead heat. No problem, Ted.

DAVE: You might be all right, Ted. Luck anyway mate. I don't think I can bear to stay.

TANNOY: Going into the traps at Monmore. At Monmore, they bet 2–1 trap 4 . . .

JANE: Dogs! Now!

TED: *(narration)* All stood there. All looking at me. Indian Jane, Big Tall Wesley, Back-pocket Dave, Mersey Billy, Formbook Povey. I could feel the pink slip in my hand. I could see their faces. I could feel my heart bang-banging in my chest. 'Apple Blossom Time'. That bloody tune. It was like a dream . . . *mum* . . .

TANNOY: Result coming from Cheltenham. The winner, number 19, 'Apple Blossom Time'; second, number 6, 'Holy Fellowship'. At Cheltenham, 'Apple Blossom Time' beat 'Holy Fellowship' in the photograph.

TED: *(narration)* Twenty thousand pounds. This Saturday in November. My birthday. And I was suddenly crying and they could all see that and looked away. Nice people. My friends at Ladbrokes. Burncross Road branch. But none of them really knew why I was crying. Not really.

TANNOY: Starting price of the winner at Cheltenham was 6–1. Distances a neck and three lengths.

The Winners

Olwen Wymark

Cast

HARRY McCOY (Master of Ceremonies)

REDCOAT I (male)

REDCOAT II (male)

REDCOAT III (female)

REDCOAT IV (female)

ROSIE (old lady)

VERA (typist)

ROGER (civil servant)

JOE (trade unionist)

CHARLES (poet)

SAMANTHA (debutante)

BARBIE (beauty queen)

DAVID (soldier)

FREDA (do-gooder)

TONY (football supporter)

BOB AND BETTY (honeymoon couple)

THE VOICE

CAMPER I

CAMPER II

CAMPER III

CAMPER IV

CAMPER V

Curtain up on darkness. Voice over a microphone accompanied by weird humming buzz.

VOICE: Listen. *(Pause.)* I am speaking to your secret self – your deep secret self. Listen. Your real self is powerful – stronger than you ever imagined. There is nothing and no-one that can stand against you. You have been chosen. Your task is victory – always victory. Anything that gets in your path must be obliterated. Listen to me. Your two best friends are your anger and your hatred. Let them be your guides. Your power must be free. Trust no-one. They are all your enemies. Crush them. Destroy them. Attack! *(Begins to fade.)* Listen. I am speaking to your secret self – your deep secret self.

Lights up on ballroom. Streamers, coloured lights, loud music. People dancing. Others standing around chatting and watching. REDCOATS *circulating and being generally jolly. The MC,* HARRY McCOY *up on the platform with microphone. Music stops. Clapping and chatter.*

HARRY: Are we all having fun?

ALL: Yes!

HARRY: Terrific, terrific – that's how I like to hear it. Remember, we've got the winners of the day coming up in a minute. Don't run away anybody–it could be you. And if you're not a winner today, you'll be one tomorrow because we're all winners here at the camp, isn't that right?

ROSIE: *(shouts)* That's right Harry!

HARRY: *(blows her a kiss)* There you go, Rosie. There's my girl. Prettiest girl in the camp, that's what you are. Get a load of those beautiful legs.

ROSIE *lifts skirts a bit and does a few dance steps. Applause – laughter.*

HARRY: Ginger Rogers! Let's dance everybody, let's dance!

Music up again. Dancing. REDCOAT I *sweeps* ROSIE *into an energetic dance. Another stands by, clapping in rhythm.* REDCOAT III *persuades* ROGER *to dance and he leads her into a stately foxtrot.*

HARRY: *(pointing at them)* Will you look at that cat go! Swing it Roger! *(Sights* VERA *standing at the side, rather awkwardly alone.)* Why aren't you dancing then, love? It's little Vera, isn't it? We can't have anybody on their ownsome lonesome. You come and cut a rug with your Uncle Harry.

He jumps off the platform, takes her hand and makes her jitterbug with him. She is laughing but embarrassed and awkward. Cut music and continue dancing in mime.

JOE: My! It's a wonder the way he remembers everybody's names.

SAMANTHA: Oh, he's divine! So friendly. Not a bit like a famous star. Mummy and I always used to watch his television show – mummy was potty about him. Remember the 'Real McCoy Show'?

JOE: I think everybody in England used to watch Harry McCoy. Highest ratings of all time, someone told me.

SAMANTHA: I wonder why he retired. I mean, he's still young.

JOE: He was saying to a few of us the other day, he thinks the television world is just plastic – unreal like. He said this kind of work is his true vocation now. Really being with people. Giving them a good time. He's a champion bloke.

SAMANTHA: But he wouldn't go to just any old holiday camp. This one's special. After all, we've all been chosen.

JOE: *(his face puzzled)* Chosen . . . *(Then nods)* Aye, that's right. We've been chosen.

Music up. Dancing continues. Then cut music and back to mime.

FREDA: Hasn't this first week gone by quickly! I'm having the time of my life. I've never been to a holiday camp before. Have you?

DAVID: No never. I wouldn't ever have thought of it if it hadn't been for the competition.

FREDA: You could have knocked me over with a feather when I won. I hadn't even sent away for that questionnaire, you know. It just arrived in the post out of the blue.

DAVID: Mine did too. I think they selected people 'specially to send it to.

FREDA: Yes. I wonder how. I only filled mine in for a joke, really. Never thought for a second I'd be one of the ones to win the free holiday. Funny sort of questions in it, weren't they?

DAVID: Well it said, didn't it? The questions were all worked out so only top ability people could get them right. Psychologically devised, they said, to pick up the basically special people.

FREDA: That's what I mean. I never dreamed there was anything special about me. Top ability! I'm just an ordinary person – just ordinary.

DAVID: Goes to show how you don't really know yourself . . . your real self.

BOTH: Your deep secret self.

They stare at each other for the briefest second. Then laugh.

FREDA: Snap!

Music up again. Then cut and back to mime

CHARLES: I never thought a holiday camp could be so exciting. I've got so much energy all the time. Do you know, I wake up every morning feeling marvellous . . . can't wait for things to start.

BARBIE: Me too. There's always so much going on. Goodness, all those races today. I nearly lost my voice cheering.

CHARLES: No, no, the races were yesterday . . . weren't they?

BARBIE: *(puzzled)* Maybe you're right. I can't seem to remember. I keep getting mixed up about what happened when.

CHARLES: It's the same for me. When I think back on this week, it's like looking into a kaleidoscope . . . everything sort of whirling around.

BARBIE: Well, it doesn't matter, does it! When you're having a good time. *(Snaps her fingers and in rhythm half sings)* Crush them! Destroy them!

CHARLES: *(joining in)* Crush them. Destroy them.

They continue for a moment or two.

BARBIE: *(laughs)* Isn't it silly, the things that come into your head? *(CHARLES laughs too.)*

Music up again and the number comes to an end. Clapping, etc.

HARRY: Are we still having fun?

ALL: Yes!

HARRY: Course we are. Top notch people having a top notch time. What a wonderful bunch. It's a real privilege being your Master of Ceremonies, I'll tell you that. It makes me feel proud and humble. And now . . . what about today's winners?

REDCOAT IV *runs up to the platform, reads out names into microphone.*

REDCOAT IV: Rosie Pringle!

ROSIE *shrieks with joy. Applause.* REDCOAT I *runs her up to the platform.* HARRY *kisses her on the cheek.*

REDCOAT IV: Roger Manning!

REDCOAT III *enthusiastically shakes* ROGER*'s hand and pushes him up to the platform. Applause.* HARRY *pats him on the back, shakes his hand.*

REDCOAT IV: Vera Grey!

VERA: *(amazed and alarmed, she has a stutter)* What? Who me?

Applause. Two REDCOATS *take her hands. She hangs back.*

HARRY: Don't be shy, Vera. Up you come.

They get her up on the platform. HARRY *hugs her.* REDCOAT IV *hands each of the three a certificate decorated with rosettes and ribbons.*

REDCOAT IV: How about a big hand for today's topnotchest topnotchers!

Applause. ROSIE *kisses her certificate.* ROGER *holds his over his head with both hands.* VERA *reads hers, her face confused.*

HARRY: How does it feel to be a winner, Rosie?

ROSIE: Grand, Harry, just grand. I always knew in my heart I could be a winner. I knew I should be. *(Fierce)* I knew it!

HARRY: Course you did. And you were right.

ROSIE: *(loud)* I was right! *(Cheers started by* REDCOAT II.*)* Thank you. Thank you all. It's the thrill of a lifetime for me. I'm sixty-nine years old, you know.

HARRY: You mean sixty-nine years young, Rosie. You're as young as you feel. *(Pats her bottom.)* And you feel pretty young to me. *(To* ROGER*)* And what about you, Roger? Surprised to be one of today's winners?

ROGER: Well, I'm very pleased, of course, Harry, but I can't say I'm surprised. I knew I'd make it. If you want to win badly enough, then you will. You have to put your heart and soul into it. *(Speaks faster)* You have to push and push hard. Don't let anything stand in your way. Never give in, nobody can stop you, don't give an inch, force your way through – you'll get there. You'll get there! *(Stops, panting a bit.)*

HARRY: Right on! *(There is another cheer.)* And now for little Vera. How are you feeling, up here with the winners?

VERA: No . . . no, I'm not . . . I didn't . . . it's a mistake . . . I can't . . . I never do . . . I didn't win. I'm not a winner.

HARRY: Isn't she a silly girl! Don't be so modest, Vera.

VERA: It's not . . . I'm not . . . don't you see . . .

HARRY: Now how could you be up here if you weren't a winner? Let me have Vera's score card for today. *(*REDCOAT IV *gives it to him.)* Wow! Will you look at that! Vera, I'll let you in on a little secret. Today you got the highest number of points anyone has had in the camp so far! The highest!

VERA: I did? Me?

HARRY: Nobody else. It's right down here in black and white. That's a record that's going to take some beating. What do you say now, Vera.

VERA: *(dazed, still stuttering)* I'm a winner. *(Stares out front for a moment. Then laughs. Speaks loud, no stutter)* I'm a a winner! I'm a winner!

Blackout. The high-pitched sound.

VOICE: Now you are moving away from the weakness of the

past. Your true reality was suffocated. Your power was sleeping. Let it wake. Let it come out from it's hiding place. Listen. The voice of your conscience is a liar. Your conscience was always your betrayer, sapping your strength, keeping your secret self a prisoner. You must be deaf to its treacherous voice. Listen to me. Feel your strength. Take up your anger like a sword. Cut through the dark jungle of illusion, up into the light, up to the mountains where you belong. Let your hatred blaze like a flame. Let your power wake. Forward! Forward! Let your power wake!

Still in darkness. Voices from different parts of the stage.

REDCOAT I: Wakey, wakey!

REDCOAT II: Rise and shine!

REDCOAT III: Everybody up. Up, up, up!

REDCOAT IV: Come on, come on! Let's have you!

Lights up on a bare stage. The REDCOATS *are standing on different parts of the stage. All the campers rush on, talking, laughing, greeting each other, etc.*

REDCOATS: Let's get started! It's a wonderful day! We don't want to waste it. Get moving, everybody, we've got a lot to do. It's time for fun. We're going to have fun *(etc.* ad lib*).*

CAMPER I: Hurry up. Why're you always so slow?

CAMPER II: Shut your face. I'm coming.

FREDA: I wonder what we'll be doing today. There's always something new. They never let you get bored, do they?

BARBIE: I hope there'll be archery again. I just loved it. It was terrifying. I thought I'd die.

FREDA: *(curious)* How do you mean . . . terrifying?

BARBIE: *(fiercely)* I wasn't scared. I never said I was scared. What the hell are you talking about?

FREDA: What?

REDCOAT I: Everybody for the karate class, over here with me.

CAMPER III: Karate? Is that the fortune-telling things you do with cards?

CAMPER IV: No, it's Japanese fighting, silly.

CAMPER III: Oh, great. Let's go.

SAMANTHA: The karate class is simply too marvellous. I was in it the other day. Are you coming?

CHARLES: No . . . no, I don't think so. I wouldn't be any good at that. I don't know how.

SAMANTHA: Anybody can do it, honestly. He's a divine teacher. I was just amazed at myself. I can't tell you how exciting it is. Come on, you'll love it. You'll be splendid at it, I promise.

CHARLES: Do you really think I would be? Oh, all right . . . yes. Yes, I will then. *(They join group round* REDCOAT I.*)*

REDCOAT II: This way, everybody who signed up for the canoeing trip. Get a move on. We want to be on our way. Over here for the canoe group.

CAMPER I: Well, come on, that's us.

CAMPER II: Don't push me . . . all right? *(They go over.)*

ROSIE: I'm on the canoeing list. I want to be in the first boat.

REDCOAT II: Well, maybe you will, Rosie. We'll wait and see.

ROSIE: *(coldly)* Maybe? What do you mean, maybe? I said I want to be first.

TONY: Are you coming in my canoe again, Vera?

VERA: No, I'm going alone. What's the matter, don't you think I can handle one by myself? That's what you think, isn't it?

TONY: I never said that.

REDCOAT II: You're all going to be solo today. We're doing something new.

CAMPER I: What? What are we going to do?

REDCOAT II: Wait and see. You're going to love it. It's paddle your own canoe day, folks. *(Laughs.)*

REDCOAT III: Come on, all you nature lovers. Where's my hiking group?

CAMPER V: Nature hike? Boring! We used to do that in school.

JOE: You won't find this boring, lad, I can guarantee you that. You might not be able to take it. You have to be pretty tough, believe me.

CAMPER V: *(annoyed)* I am tough. *(Joins group.)*

DAVID: Really rugged, is it?

JOE: Aye, it is that. I went on the last one. Never experienced anything like it in my life.

DAVID: Why? What did you do?

JOE: Well we . . . what we did was . . . I can't rightly describe it . . . but we had a champion time. Why don't you come and see for yourself?

DAVID: *(as they join group)* Right. If it's tough, that's for me.

REDCOAT IV: Over here for sports. Badminton, archery, bowling . . . this way for sports.

BARBIE: Oh, goody. You coming too?

FREDA: I'm not very good at sports, actually.

BARBIE: *(surprised)* That doesn't matter. Come on.

ROGER: You free? I need a partner for badminton. My partner broke his leg.

CAMPER IV: How'd he do that?

ROGER: God knows. He was just bloody stupid *(They join group.)*

REDCOATS: Everybody set? Let's get going, gang. We're wasting fun time, folks. Let's get this show on the road.

CAMPER II: I don't know where my life-jacket is.

FREDA: I'm not sure I want to do sports. I don't know what I want to do.

TONY: God, I'm tired. I wouldn't mind going back to bed for a bit.

CAMPER V: Yeah, me too. I don't feel like doing anything.

A kind of general, negative murmer runs through the group.

REDCOATS: *(overlapping each other, commanding tones)* Forward! Forward! Forward! Forward!

The group freezes for a second. Then breaks into enthusiastic sound.

VARIOUS VOICES: What are we waiting for? Let's get a move on. Let's go, let's go, let's go! *(etc.* ad lib*).*

And they all surge off the stage, laughing and talking. HARRY McCOY *walks on from the other side after they've gone. He stands looking after them. The lights dim. After a moment, the karate group comes on towards him. They look exhausted.* CHARLES *is limping, his arm around* SAMANTHA*'s neck and she's helping him along.*

HARRY: *(very cheery)* Hello there! It's the karate class, isn't it? How'd you get on, bunch? Have a good day?

CHARLES: I've got a complaint!

HARRY: *(amazed)* Complaint, Charles? What's the trouble? What's the problem? Didn't you enjoy it? Didn't you have fun today? What's up then?

CHARLES: The morning session was fine – I liked it. It was much easier than I thought. I was pretty good but . . .

HARRY: Great, Charles, terrific! I knew you would be.

CHARLES: But this afternoon it all went crazy. *(His voice rises)* You're supposed to work in pairs. That's what we'd been *doing*! And then all of a sudden they *all* turned on me! Every one of them.

SAMANTHA: But, Charles, you don't understand.

CHARLES: No, I bloody well don't. You all just went for me. Six against one. It wasn't fair.

HARRY: *(keen)* So what did you do, Charles? Did you fight back?

CHARLES: I had to! I had to protect myself.

HARRY: That's wonderful, Charles. Congratulations.

SAMANTHA: He was simply too marvellous. He was like a tiger.

CAMPER III: We nearly got him, though.

CAMPER IV: It was really something.

SAMANTHA: It was incredible, Harry. I wish you could have seen it.

HARRY: I wish I could've too, Samantha, it sounds wild. That's just fantastic, Charles. I knew you had it in you.

CHARLES: But wait a minute, I . . .

REDCOAT I: *(who has been watching comes up)* He was absolutely first class. Talk about a topnotcher! You don't often see work like that. I was very proud of you, Charles. Very, very proud.

CHARLES: You were?

HARRY: Course he was. And so am I. Well done, Charles!

CHARLES: Oh, well . . . thanks, Harry . . . I

HARRY: I guess we know who one of today's winners is going to be.

CHARLES: Gosh . . . I never thought I'd . . .

REDCOAT I: Don't know what you can do 'til you do it, do you, Charles? I was proud of them all, Harry. They're just amazing, every last one of them. We've got a few little cuts and bruises . . . a couple of sprains.

HARRY: Well, go on over to the infirmary, all of you, and get yourselves fixed up. Hurry back – the barbecue's going to be ready soon.

REDCOAT I: This way, champs. *(He leads them off.)*

SAMANTHA: *(as they go)* Oooh, you are lucky, Charles. I wish I'd been the one. Wasn't it exciting?

CHARLES: Yes, it was. I've never felt like that before. He's right. You really don't know what you can do 'til you do it.

SAMANTHA: *(laughing)* If only Mummy could see me now!

The stage darkens further until there is only an area of light round HARRY. *The other* REDCOATS *join him in the light, standing round him and facing out. The rest of the* CAMPERS *come on from various directions in the dark.*

CAMPER I: What a day!

HARRY: Yeah?

CAMPER II: The best one yet!

HARRY: Good!

CAMPER III: We really clobbered those stupid bastards.

REDCOAT I: You really did!

JOE: Not one of them could touch me in that cave. I'm not saying I wasn't scared, but not as scared as they were.

REDCOAT II: I bet they were.

ROSIE: I rammed more canoes than anybody else! I broke one! Broke it in pieces!

REDCOAT III: Attagirl!

DAVID: What about that hunt! God, you should have heard that woman scream. *(Laughs.)*

REDCOAT IV: *(laughs)* Terrific!

ROGER: I've never played badminton with a live bird before. It's smashing! *(Laughs.)*

HARRY: *(laughs)* Smashing!

FREDA: They all looked so stupid!

REDCOAT: That's what they are!

TONY: I crashed right into him!

REDCOAT: That's the way to do it.

BARBIE: She never stood a chance!

REDCOAT: No sir!

JOE: At 'em and at 'em! You have to keep at 'em!

REDCOAT: Keep at 'em!

HARRY: Are you all having fun?

ALL: Yes!

REDCOAT: Are you all winners?

ALL: Yes!

REDCOAT: Can anybody stop you?

ALL: No!

REDCOAT: Are you going to the top?

ALL: Yes!

The high-pitched sound. Complete stillness on stage.

VOICE: *(quietly)* You have been chosen.

Another moment's silence. Then

REDCOAT: *(at back of stage)* Come and get it! The bonfire's lit and the food's all ready.

An orange spot lights up a biggish circle upstage. Light on HARRY *and* REDCOATS *exit.*

REDCOAT: Barbecue time. Round the bonfire everybody.

All move up and sit in a semicircle on the edge of the orange area, with their backs to the audience. The REDCOATS *circulate, miming giving out food, etc.* HARRY *leads off into a song and they all join in.*

REDCOAT III: Who's that?

BOB *and* BETTY *have come on downstage, carrying flashlights.*

REDCOAT II: Stop right there!

The singing tapers off. The campers turn to look and slowly stand up. The four REDCOATS *converge swiftly on the two figures.* HARRY *stands watching.*

REDCOAT IV: Turn those torches on your faces.

REDCOAT I: Now! We want to see you.

The two turn their lights onto their faces.

BOB: Wait a minute. What's wrong? We . . .

REDCOAT I: What are you doing here?

REDCOAT II: How did you get in?

REDCOAT III: No-one's allowed in here without a pass.

BETTY: But we have a pass.

BOB: I've got it right here.

REDCOAT IV: What are your names?

BOB: Black. Bob and Betty Black.

REDCOAT II: No latecomers are allowed.

REDCOAT I: It's against the rules.

REDCOAT IV: You'll have to get out.

BETTY: But we've got a letter from Harry McCoy. Show them, Bob.

BOB: What is all this, anyway? We're not criminals.

REDCOAT III: Over here. Come on. Over here.

They hustle them up to where HARRY *is standing.*

HARRY: Wait a minute. Wait a minute. What's all the hassle? I know who these two are . . . you're the newlyweds, aren't you?

BETTY: Yes. Yes, we are. His mum and dad won the competition but they gave us their places for a wedding present.

BOB: We had special permission to come a week late.

HARRY: That's right. Of course you did. I remember. No need for any bother. Welcome to the camp. This is Bob and Betty Black, everybody. The new Mister and Missus.

General greetings.

REDCOAT I: Sorry about that, Bob. We always have to be on the look-out for gatecrashers.

REDCOAT II: Everybody wants to get in here, you know. Didn't mean to upset you, Betty.

BETTY: *(nervously)* Oh, that's all right.

BOB: Forget it. We understand.

HARRY: That's the way. All friends now, eh?

REDCOAT II: What about a kiss from the bride? *(Kisses her, applause.)*

REDCOAT IV: And one for me from the groom. *(Kisses him.)* Equal rights!

ROSIE: How long have you two been married?

BOB: *(looks at his watch)* Seven hours, twenty-eight minutes and four seconds.

CAMPERS: Oooh . . . lovely . . . congratulations . . . *(etc.* ad lib).

FREDA: Would you like some supper? There's a lot of food left.

BOB: No thanks, we stopped on the way for a meal.

ROGER: Food? They don't want food. It's their wedding night.

TONY: Yeah, what they want is a good night's sleep.

HARRY: Oh, what a crude lot you are. But joking apart, you all need your beddy-byes. You've had a busy, busy day.

REDCOAT II: And tomorrow's going to be even busier, gang.

REDCOAT III: It's Kiddies Games Day tomorrow.

REDCOAT IV: We want you all raring to go in the morning.

REDCOAT I: Fun and games non-stop all day. Lots of points to be won.

HARRY: And it won't be child's play. You're going to need all the energy you've got. Everybody off to the land of nod, eh?

BARBIE: Let's give Bob and Betty an escort party to their chalet.

HARRY: Good idea. A wedding parade.

BOB *and* BETTY *are lifted onto shoulders. Someone starts humming, 'Here Comes the Bride' and the others join in, as they go off and the lights fade.*

This changes to a group offstage singing, 'Oranges and Lemons', as the lights come up to full on the stage. REDCOAT II *runs on with another group of campers. Sets up 'Cat and Mouse'. Has loud whistle for changeover. The game goes very quickly. Offstage, when the song reaches 'Here comes a chopper to chop off your head' a man shouts 'Don't! Don't!', followed by laughter. Then onstage,* REDCOAT II *blows the whistle and the group goes into a circle, in which the Cat and Mouse are trapped together. The Cat starts to laugh as he goes for the Mouse, who runs about trying to get out, panic stricken. The circle closes in, the whole group shouting frenziedly. Then the whistle, and the circle breaks up immediately.* REDCOAT II *and the others congratulate the Cat. The Mouse lies in a heap on the floor, moaning. Nobody pays any attention to him, and as they all go off, people step over him as if he weren't there. Then he crawls offstage, still moaning. Offstage, a group has started singing, 'London Bridge'. Onstage comes a group of four girls and a man, with* REDCOAT I *. They play a spirited game of 'What's the Time, Mr Wolf' while the singing goes on offstage until we hear a girl scream, 'I can't, I can't, I'll fall', and other voices saying, 'Go on, go on, push her', etc. And there is a scream, followed by cheers. At which point Mr Wolf turns on one of the girls, knocks her down and* *starts to throttle her. This could be done in silence with the other girls watching and* REDCOAT I *standing beside the struggling couple, calmly marking a score card. Then* REDCOAT I *leans down and taps Mr Wolf on the shoulder smartly. He leaps up immediately and the girls and* REDCOAT I *shake his hand, etc. The victim goes off, having tried and failed to make contact with the others, who ignore her. Then, two* REDCOATS *run on, carrying a bench and miming carrying two pillows. They shout,* 'Pillow Fight' *and all the campers come on. They place the bench and two people get up on it and bash each other with the pillows, 'til one of them falls, the others standing upstage, cheering. This goes on until it is* BOB *and* BETTY *facing each other. They start with the pillows, laughing and clowning a bit, and then the two* REDCOATS *go and mime picking up two swords. They come to* BOB *and* BETTY *, grab their pillows and give them the swords.* BOB *and* BETTY *look uncertainly at the swords for a moment. Sudden silence. The high-pitched sound and the* VOICE *saying,* 'The sword of your anger'. *Then there is a huge shout from the crowd and the two start fighting. The crowd continue to shout and gesture but in complete silence.* BETTY *knocks* BOB *off the bench, he drops his sword and falls on the floor. She's over him immediately holding her sword up over him with both her hands. The crowd stands still, watching. She raises the sword and at once one of the* REDCOATS *knocks it neatly out of her hands. The crowd groans in angry protest.*

REDCOAT I: *(laughs, wags his finger at them)* Greedy! *(To* BOB *and* BETTY*)* Well done, you two! Marvellous!

REDCOAT II: Great! Really great! And it's only your first day.

HARRY *runs on clapping his hands.*

HARRY: Last game. 'Hide and seek'. Come on, Barbie. You're going to be it.

BARBIE: Oh good!

He leads her upstage and places her back to the audience. She puts her hands over her eyes and starts counting. Everyone runs off. Cut all light except a spot on BARBIE *and* HARRY, *who is whispering to her.*

BARBIE: *(laughs)* Yes! Yes! I will!

He goes off. She stands, silently counting.

BARBIE: . . . ninety-four, ninety-five, ninety-six, ninety-seven, ninety-eight, ninety-nine, one hundred. *(Takes her hands down, turns, arms out. Shouts loudly and rather wildly)* Ready or not, here I come!

She runs off. Blackout. High-pitched sound.

VOICE: I am always with you. You cannot hide from me. I am lodged deep in your centre forever . . . the centre of your self. Forget about laws and rules. Those are for slaves. You are your own rule. Listen to me. My words beat in your heart, sing in your blood. I am always with you.

REDCOAT I: *(offstage)* Olly, olly, oxen free. I'm free! I'm free!

Others take up this call.

BARBIE: I want to go on! Let go of me, I want to go on!

REDCOAT II: Not now, Barbie. Game's over.

HARRY: Is everybody here?

REDCOAT III: Think so.

VERA: Tony isn't here.

REDCOAT IV: Where is he? Has anybody seen Tony?

General 'No's and ad libs.

HARRY: Divide into search parties immediately. Go out and look for him.

Lights up to dim on stage. HARRY *and the* REDCOATS *come on from different directions. Offstage, we hear voices calling* TONY.

REDCOAT I: Anybody find him?

OTHERS: No.

REDCOAT III: Anything can happen. I told you 'Hide and Seek' was risky, Harry.

HARRY: All right! I didn't think this would happen, did I?

REDCOAT IV: We're wasting time. We'll have to check the outer gates.

They go off. TONY *comes running on.* BOB *enters downstage, sees him.*

BOB: Tony! Everybody's looking for you. Haven't you heard them calling?

TONY: Get out of my way! Get out of my way!

He stumbles, nearly falls, BOB *catches him.*

BOB: What's wrong, mate? What's the matter?

TONY: *(incoherent)* I have to get out of here . . . let me go . . . it's all . . . I have to . . . it's crazy, it's crazy! I'm scared . . . let me go . . . I can't stay here.

BOB: Calm down, Tony, relax. What's happened?

TONY: I can't trust you . . . I'm not supposed to trust anybody . . . I know that . . . I'm strong . . . I know, I know! . . . my power . . . nothing can stop my power . . . I believe it . . . I can hear it all the time . . . all the time . . . but now, tonight, I heard them. I heard them talking . . . I . . . oh God, I'm all mixed up.

BOB: Just tell me what happened. Heard who talking?

TONY: *(grabbing him, very intense)* Listen to me! Listen. I know you won't believe me but there's something wrong about them . . . there's something wrong going on here.

BOB: I do believe you. My God, I've seen it. I've been

completely confused. I thought nobody realised. They all seemed so happy.

TONY: *(suddenly rather cold)* Happy? Of course they're happy. They're all winners, aren't they? You wouldn't understand.

BOB: Wait a minute. You said there was something wrong. What the hell is up with you, Tony? You said you heard somebody talking. Who?

TONY: *(stares into his face for a moment, then closes his eyes)* I can't get it straight. I can't keep it straight in my head. *(Then as if forcing himself, his eyes still shut, speaking rapidly)* I was going to hide in one of the little caves. I must have hit my head on something. I don't remember. But I knocked myself out. When I came to . . . I . . . I . . . I . . . *(Stops. Then pushes himself on.)* It was dark and I had this pain in my head. I felt dizzy. I heard them calling me. I was going to call back but then two of the Redcoats went by. I heard them . . . they were talking . . . I heard it . . . I . . . I . . . I . . . I . . . *(Opens his eyes. Pulls away.)* I want to get out of here.

BOB: *(restraining him)* What did they say?

TONY: You think I'm crazy, don't you? You think I've gone off my head.

BOB: No, I don't. I don't. Just tell me what they said.

TONY: *(looks round nervously, speaks low)* It wasn't what they said . . . it was the way they said it. They're doing something to all of us in this camp . . . They're changing us . . . I couldn't understand it . . . I was so confused and my head was sort of pounding, but I knew! I knew! *(Struggles.)* Let me go. I have to get away.

BOB: Tony, you couldn't get out now. Everybody's looking for you.

TONY: Oh God, what am I going to do?

BOB: *(firm)* Now listen. What you have to do is tell the others what you've told me. Then we can all get together and find out what is going on.

TONY: *(muttering, nodding, still dazed)* Yes. Yes, you're right. Talk to them. Yes. They've all got to be warned.

BOB: But we have to be careful. Come on, we'll go and tell Harry you're found. *(TONY hangs back.)* Come on, Tony, don't be afraid.

TONY: *(loud, angry)* Afraid? What do you mean, afraid? Who the hell do you think you are? I . . . *(Stops. Closes eyes for a moment. Opens them. Looks round wildly.)* I . . . I . . . I . . .

BOB: *(gently)* Tony. Come on. I'm with you, okay? *(Takes him by the arm.)*

TONY: *(submissive)* Okay.

BOB: *(as they go out)* Then tomorrow, you can just go round and talk to people on the quiet, yes?

TONY: *(sounding exhausted)* Yes . . . yes . . . yes.

Lights up from dim to bright onstage. Enter BARBIE *with* TONY *. They walk across stage as they talk.*

BARBIE: *(impatient)* Look, do you mind. I'm going to the swimming-pool. I do twenty lengths a day to keep in shape.

TONY: Have you heard anything I've been saying?

BARBIE: Well, you're being so boring! Rabbiting on and on like that. I'm too busy to listen to you. Haven't you got anything better to do than go around boring people?

TONY: Barbie, they're trying to change us. Will you listen?

BARBIE: *(not looking at him or really noticing him, as she talks)* Change? Of course, I'm changing. I've been changing the whole time. Oh, things are going to be different, believe me. I didn't know what I could do. I've won seven beauty contests, you know, but that's not enough for me. Oh no. Nothing's enough for me now. I'm going for Miss World and Miss Universe. *(Laughs.)* They won't be able to stop me. They'll try but they don't know anything about anything. They don't *know* who I am!

By which time she is off. CHARLES *has come on.* TONY *goes to him.*

TONY: Listen, Charles. I want to tell you something.

CHARLES: Well, I'm rather busy, actually. I know I don't look as if I am but as a matter of fact I'm trying to work out a poem. Did you know I was a poet?

TONY: Well, yes but . . .

CHARLES: People always think poets are silly and vague . . . head in the clouds, you know. Well, they're wrong. Poets can be fantastically important. Strong? My God! People are so stupid. They don't really understand anything.

TONY: Look, what I'm trying to tell you is there's something going on in this camp. They're trying to change us. They . . .

CHARLES: *(very serious)* Oh, you don't have to tell me.

TONY: You know?

CHARLES: *(laughs)* Know! My god, yes! And I'm so grateful. I can't get over it. I had no idea what I was really like. Can you believe it? Oh, to be stretched like this in this amazing way. To be opened up like this . . . to be . . . well, it may sound arrogant, but honestly . . . to be transformed the way I have been.

TONY: Transformed . . . that's what I mean! The things that Harry and the Redcoats . . .

CHARLES: Oh, incredible, I know. You're right. Tony. They're simply stupendous people. Nobody's ever had that kind of faith in me before. Would you like to hear how far I've got with this poem?

TONY: Charles, please listen.

CHARLES: Of course, Tony. Of course, I will. *(Immediately starts intoning his poem.)*

Out of the night that covers me,
Black as the Pit from pole to pole,
I thank whatever gods may be
For my unconquerable soul.

Beyond this place of wrath and tears
Looms but the Horror of the shade
And yet the menace of the years . . .

Then I thought I'd finish on the image of a space missile. I need something that communicates both the death feeling and the terrific speed, you see.

By which time he is off and TONY *has given up anyway and approached* ROSIE, *who has come on.*

ROSIE: *(laughing)* I have no idea what you mean; no idea in the world. Oh, you're such a cute boy. If I was fifty years younger, you wouldn't get away from me.

TONY: Rosie, what I'm talking about is the way we all keep doing things we don't know we're going to do.

ROSIE: You're simply adorable. Now, somebody told me that you're a football hooligan.

TONY: No, I'm . . .

ROSIE: Oh, I love them, I love them, I love them. Tearing down the goalposts, throwing bottles at people, smashing up trains. It's so thrilling. Nothing stops them. Will you take me to a match one day? I'd love to do all those things.

TONY: Rosie, if you'd just . . .

ROSIE: Know what I'm doing today? Chopping wood for the bonfire. Feel those biceps. *(She thrusts an arm into his face. He pinches her biceps.)* Like iron, aren't they? Well, I'm off. Lovely chat, ducky.

And she's gone, and BOB *enters. He and* TONY *meet in the middle.*

TONY: They won't listen. They don't even seem to hear me.

BOB: Maybe one at a time is no good. Maybe you should talk to some of them when they're together. There's a group in the gym now. Let's go there. *(As they go)* I'll get the Redcoat out of there.

Enter FREDA, VERA, SAMANTHA, TONY, JOE *and* DAVID . *The stage is now the gym. They start doing press-ups, weight-lifting, skipping rope, etc.* REDCOAT I *has followed them in and goes round individually coaching.* BOB *enters.*

REDCOAT I: Good morning. Another body-builder?

BOB: Well no, I just wanted to report that the loudspeaker in our chalet seems to have broken down.

REDCOAT I: Oh, yeah? That's bad. I'll come and have a look. *(To others)* Keep at it. When I come back we'll go out for our run.

Exit REDCOAT I *and* BOB.

TONY: Can I talk to you for a minute?

SAMANTHA: You sound as if you're going to make a speech.

TONY: No . . . it's just . . . there's something I want to say.

ROGER: We've only got fifteen minutes' workout before we go running. Can't it keep?

TONY: No, it can't. It's important.

DAVID: Well, what is it? Get on with it.

They stop doing whatever they're doing and gather round him.

TONY: What it is . . . *(He stops.)*

FREDA: Go on. What it is, is what?

TONY: *(blurting it out)* There's something happening to us here. Something bad.

JOE: Something bad? What are you blathering about?

TONY: They're changing us. Harry . . . the Redcoats . . . I don't know how . . . I don't even know what it is, but they're . . . they're controlling us.

VERA: Harry? Are you out of your mind?

SAMANTHA: How on earth could they 'control' us? What an utterly loony thing to say.

TONY: I said, I didn't know how. But you've all seen . . . you must have . . . I mean, everything we do here ends in some kind of aggro . . . people getting hurt.

ROGER: Oh, for God's sake, Tony. A few little accidents. And it's all just carelessness . . . stupid idiots.

JOE: Anyway, those people should never have been here in the first place. They're not real winners, that lot.

FREDA: And they know it, you know. I go and see them in the infirmary every day . . . hospital visiting's one of my hobbies . . . and they won't even talk to you. They won't even look you in the face because they're ashamed of being so feeble . . . and so they should be.

ROGER: Maybe you shouldn't be here either, Tony. You're sounding a bit feeble yourself.

DAVID: Yeah, who are you, anyway? You're just a little nobody. I mean, what do you do? You work in an office and you're a football supporter. Nothing very important about that. I wonder why they let you in.

TONY: *(suddenly angry)* Just watch it, David. You think you're important just because you're going into the army? You'll only be a lousy private.

DAVID: Listen, mate. I'm going into the SAS, and don't you forget it. Little thugs like you are going to have to watch out for me.

TONY: *(with an effort)* Look. Wait. I'm not talking about whether anyone's important. That doesn't matter. It doesn't matter. Vera, you work in an office too, don't you?

VERA: Not like you. I'm taking over that office. That's the plan. I'll be director. What do you mean, it doesn't matter? It's what matters most. We are important.

SAMANTHA: Look at Roger. He's terribly high up in the civil service.

ROGER: *(grimly)* And going to be a lot higher.

SAMANTHA: And I don't suppose you think a London debutante is very important but I can assure you, it can jolly well be a corridor of power. And it's going to be for me.

TONY: Oh please, listen . . . *(But nobody does.)*

FREDA: Oh, now . . . I feel a bit of a fool. I mean, I am nobody. I'm not important at all.

JOE: No, that's wrong, Freda.

FREDA: Oh Joe, we all know how influential you are in the trades unions and that's just the beginning for you. You've said so. But me? I'm just a little voluntary social worker . . . meals on wheels, prison visiting, a spot of marriage guidance counselling, the Samaritans . . . just a little nobody, bobbing about trying to do some good in the world.

JOE: Freda, what was Harry saying to you the other day? All the people you come into contact with are in a very vulnerable state, right?

FREDA: Well, yes, that is true.

JOE: Which means that your influence can be crucial.

FREDA: Yes. *(Laughs)* Yes, I see that.

TONY: Will anybody listen to me?

DAVID: Yes! I'll listen. I'd like to know what the hell it is you're saying about Harry and the Redcoats. For my money, they're pretty bloody fantastic people, and they work their guts out for us. The discipline in this place is very, very good. So just what are you on about?

TONY: If you'll just listen! Last night, I heard two of the Redcoats talking. They didn't know I was there.

JOE: Go on. Talking about what? What did they say?

TONY: I can't remember exactly what it was they said . . . No, wait. After I'd heard them, I knew . . . I knew for certain that they're using us for something. They've got us in their power.

SAMANTHA: You *are* crazy. Got us in their power? Us?

ROGER: *(simply)* You know that's impossible.

VERA: *(contemptuous)* That must have been some bang you got on the head last night. It's made your brains go funny.

FREDA: That's it. Of course. You didn't hear anything, Tony. It was just because you hit your head. You imagined it.

TONY: *(bit shaken)* No . . . no, I'm sure I . . . I know . . .

JOE: Aye, of course. That'll be it.

SAMANTHA: Like a hallucination. You were delirious.

ROGER: Well-known medical fact, that sort of thing happens with mild concussion.

TONY: *(confused)* But . . . but . . .

ROGER: It's the only explanation, man. Pull yourself together. You can see how absolutely ludicrous it is. *(Starts to laugh)* Harry and the Redcoats controlling us?

FREDA: *(laughing)* Having us in their power? It's like science fiction.

DAVID: *(laughing)* As if we were all a bunch of robots.

They all laugh together. TONY *is very confused now.*

TONY: Hang on. Wait . . . wait. I told Bob about it last night. He thinks there's something strange going on here. He said that.

VERA: Bob? He's not even one of us.

FREDA: Didn't you hear Betty say? They didn't win the competition, you know.

SAMANTHA: They don't belong here. I don't think they should have been let in.

JOE: Harry gave them permission and Harry knows what he's doing. Bob's jealous. That's all it'll be.

DAVID: Yeah, because he knows there's no way he can be a winner.

ROGER: You don't want to bother about him. He's a nobody.

VERA: I don't know, though. If he's going around talking like that. *(Vituperative)* He ought to be taught a lesson.

FREDA: Vera's right! who the hell does he think he is, spreading disgusting rumours like that?

TONY: But he didn't. I . . .

JOE: Was he or was he not talking against Harry and the Redcoats?

TONY: Well, yes, he was but . . . oh God, it's all mixed up in my head now.

SAMANTHA: Don't you see? He was taking advantage of you because you were mixed up. Your head and everything, and getting lost. He's sneaky. And he's a troublemaker.

DAVID: We should warn Harry about him.

ROGER: We know what Harry would want us to do. Like Vera says, teach him a lesson. *(All agree.)* Tony?

TONY: I . . . I don't know.

JOE: Now then, lad, let's sort this thing out. You know perfectly well that every single one of us is special, don't you? We *know* that. You didn't know what you were saying. We're all aware that you were a winner four times running in the first week. You, of all people, must see that nobody could control us *because* we're special. You do see that?

TONY: *(bemused)* Yes . . .

FREDA: And you know that Harry and the Redcoats are the best friends we've ever had.

TONY: Yes . . .

DAVID: Nobody can stand in our way, right?

TONY: Right.

SAMANTHA: Nobody can make *us* do anything, right?

TONY: Right.

VERA: *We* make our *own* rules, right?

TONY: *(strong)* Right! *(Puts his hand over his eyes for a moment. Then laughs.)* You're right. Of course, you're right.

ROGER: Right! There's no problem, then. All we do is get Bob.

DAVID: What'll we do to him?

FREDA: Look out, he's coming.

ROGER: We'll think of something.

Enter BOB *and* REDCOAT II.

REDCOAT II: All ready for the run, you chaps? You with us, Bob?

BOB: No . . . I don't think so.

DAVID: *(under his breath)* Too true.

BOB: You coming with me, Tony?

TONY: *(not looking at him)* I'm going running.

BOB: Oh . . . I thought we . . .

TONY: *(looks at him with dislike)* I'm going running.

REDCOAT II: *(goes to* TONY, *puts friendly arm round him)* You sure, Tony? That was quite a nasty knock you got last night. Maybe you should rest today.

TONY: *(smiles at him)* I'll be all right. I'll take it easy.

REDCOAT II: Well, good for you, Tony. True grit, eh? Congratulations.

TONY: Thanks.

BOB: Tony . . could I have a word with you?

TONY *hesitates then goes slowly over to him. The others watch.*

BOB: *(low)* Did you warn them?

TONY: Look, just leave me alone, will you? And listen . . . you'd better watch out.

BOB: What? *(Puts hand on* TONY*'s arm.)* Why are you . . .?

TONY: *(flings his hand off, walks back to others)* I'm busy, okay?

BOB: I don't get it.

TONY: *(laughs)* You will. *(The others laugh with him.)*

REDCOAT II: What's up?

TONY: Just a joke.

REDCOAT II: All merry and bright, eh? That's the way we like it. Well, come on, team. Let's hit the old track. *(He runs in place and the others follow suit.)* So long, Bob.

OTHERS: *(very bright)* Bye, Bob. Be seeing you, Bob. Ta ta for now, Bob. *(And they all run off.)*

Blackout. In the dark, a few people run on and scatter chairs and things. There is the sound of breaking glass, people talking in hoarse whispers, thumping, etc. Then silence. Then a scream. Lights up on BETTY*, standing in the middle of the mess, in a square of light which is her and* BOB*'s chalet.* FREDA, BARBIE, CHARLES *and* DAVID *stand outside the chalet, as if looking through windows.*

BETTY: Oh my God! Why? Why? All our things. *(Moves around picking up things and helplessly letting them fall again.)* My clothes! They're all ripped up. *(Starts to cry.)* I don't understand. *(Kneels on the floor.)* All my perfume . . . my make-up . . . it's all smashed up. Who would do this? What am I going to do? *(Hugs herself and shivers. Looks up at the walls.)* They've broken all the windows. *(Gets up and moves towards a window.)* Oh, Bob, where are you? Bob . . . Bob . . . *(Then startled)* Who's there?

FREDA: Gosh, Betty, what have you been up to?

BARBIE: *(giggling)* What a mess!

DAVID: Been having a row with hubby, Betty?

CHARLES: Or a nervous breakdown? *(They all laugh.)*

BETTY: What are you talking about? Somebody's wrecked our chalet. Look at it! Can't you see? Why are you all laughing? *(Stops.)* Was it you?

BARBIE: Us? Goodness, no.

CHARLES: What a thing to say.

DAVID: We're your friends, Betty.

FREDA: Oh look, here comes somebody. Maybe they'll know.

VERA *and* ROGER *enter and come up to chalet.*

ROGER: *(very hearty)* Well . . . surprised, Betty?

VERA: What do you think of it?

BETTY: Did you do this?

VERA: Well, not just us. There were quite a few of us. Wow! We did quite a job.

ROGER: Not bad. Considering it was all in the dark. Pretty splendid, really.

BETTY: But why? Why did you do it? How could you?

VERA: *(casual)* Oh, it was Bob's idea.

BETTY: *(aghast)* *Bob*?

ROGER: Honeymoon prank, you know. He thought it would be quite a scream.

BARBIE: It was!

CHARLES: You should have heard her. Some scream. Sensational! *(Laughs.)*

BETTY: I don't believe you! He wouldn't! It isn't true.

ROSIE, TONY, JOE *and* SAMANTHA *enter and stroll over.*

VERA: Rosie, tell Betty. Whose idea was this?

ROSIE: Bob's, of course. *(Peers in.)* Gracious to Heaven, isn't that a sight!

SAMANTHA: Betty's crying! Honestly, Betty, I thought you were a good sport.

JOE: *(interested)* She looks frightened. *(Goes towards her.)* Frightened, Betty?

BETTY: Don't touch me.

JOE: *(contemptuous)* I don't want to touch you.

TONY: Bob said you were a bit of a dead loss in the old touching department *(Everyone laughs.)*

DAVID: He said you were a bit of an old slag, actually.

BETTY: He didn't say that. He didn't, he didn't!

FREDA: *(judicious)* How long did you know Bob before you got married, Betty?

BETTY: A month. *(Angrily)* What's it to you?

FREDA: Oh, nothing. It's just the way he talks about you. I've got a feeling he may well be the wife-beater type. I do a lot of counselling, you know. I can usually tell.

BARBIE: Oh, he's said some terrible things about you, Betty. *(Giggles)* I couldn't repeat them.

BETTY: You're all lying to me.

ROSIE: *(laughs)* Marry in haste, repent at leisure.

BETTY: Shut up! Shut up! Shut up!

DAVID: Why are you getting so hysterical, Betty? I guess Bob was right when he said you were really neurotic.

VERA: Freaky. She hasn't got any self-discipline, that's her trouble.

ROGER: *(seriously)* You say we're lying to you because you can't face the truth. But it is true, Betty, it really is.

BETTY: *(staring at him)* No . . . no . . .

BOB *enters and comes up to the group.*

BOB: What's up? Is something wrong? Betty!

BETTY: Don't come in here! Don't come near me! I hate you! How could you, how could you?

BOB: How could I what? What're you talking about? *(The group that's crowded round the door, parts.)* My God! What's happened? Who did this?

BETTY: How dare you say that, how dare you? You! You told them to do it.

They all laugh in a comfortable kind of way and move back, watching.

BOB: Me? Me tell them to . . . *(Looks at them)* What've you been telling her?

SAMANTHA: Only the truth, Bob. How you thought it would be funny if we smashed up your chalet.

CHARLES: Didn't we do a great job? You pleased?

BOB: Funny! You're all crazy. You're mad.

TONY: *(fierce)* Watch your mouth!

BOB: *(lunging at him)* By God, I'll get you!

DAVID: *(grabbing* BOB *and twisting his arm behind his back)* Oh, I don't think you're going to get anybody, Bob.

BARBIE: What an actor! Look at him . . . the innocent hero. Wonderful, Bob!

ROSIE: You ought to go on the stage.

BETTY: Get him! Why doesn't one of you get Bob? Beat him up!

BOB: Betty, don't!

VERA: Why don't you get him, Betty?

DAVID: Yeah. Come on, Betty. I'll hold him.

They all egg her on. Then silence as BETTY *starts to move towards* BOB.

BETTY: You thought it would funny! You thought it would be a scream. You're the one who'll scream. So I'm a slag, am I? Neurotic? You'll see how neurotic I can be. *(With hatred)* I'll scratch your eyes out.

BOB: Stop! Betty, listen to me!

JOE: *(as she nearly reaches* BOB*)* Oh, let him go.

DAVID: Okay. *(Gives* BOB*'s arm final twist and lets him fall.)*

SAMANTHA: What's wrong, Betty? Why are you so upset and everything?

BARBIE: Bob's trying to say something to you. Why won't you listen? After all, he is your husband.

BETTY: *(staring round the group)* What . . . what . . .

BOB: Betty . . .

CHARLES: Go on, Bob. She needs calming down. Goodness!

BOB: *(ignoring him, intensely to* BETTY*)* I did not tell them to do this. I never said one word against you. I love you.

FREDA: Oooh, sweet!

ROSIE: So romantic!

BOB: Do you believe me, Betty?

DAVID: Do you believe him, Betty?

BETTY: *(covers her face with her hands)* I don't know what to believe. They all said . . . they told me you . . .

ROGER: *(casual)* Oh, that was just a joke.

BOB: But why?

JOE: Just a bit of fun.

BOB: Tony, you tell me why.

TONY: *(unpleasant)* You know why.

BETTY *starts to cry again.* BOB *moves to put his arms round her. She backs away.*

BETTY: Don't come near me. I don't want you near me.

FREDA: Don't worry, Bob. *(Laughs.)* All marriages have their little ups and downs, you know.

Someone mockingly hums a couple of phrases from 'Here Comes the Bride'. Blackout, as they all laugh. They go off and clear the stage. The high-pitched sound. In the blackout and under cover of the following, HARRY *and* REDCOATS *set up the conference area on the other side of the stage.*

VOICE: The time is nearly here. The power is about to blaze out of you. You can feel it pulsing and beating inside you. You have done well . . . Soon, there will be nothing that you cannot do. You have burned the weakness and the lazy softness out of yourself. Your will is white hot. You are pure and ruthless; hard and bright as a diamond. Soon . . . soon you will begin to move. If anyone tries to stop you, trample them like slugs, crush them like vermin – like the filth that they are. Violence is clean. Violence is victory.

Lights up on conference area. REDCOATS *sitting at table.* HARRY *downstage, standing up and facing out. They are all in listening attitudes.*

VOICE: *(now on smaller tannoy accoustic)* Let your violence ring like a great bell, strike like lightning, crash like deafening thunder. Violence is victory. Remember what I have told you. Violence is victory. Remember.

Voice stops. HARRY *reaches up and mimes switching off speaker. There is a click.*

REDCOAT I: *(shaking head admiringly)* It's very good, isn't it? it? It's really very good.

REDCOAT II: Do you know, sometimes when I'm on the night shift, listening to that stuff, I can actually feel it working on *me*. *(Shivers very slightly.)* It's a funny feeling.

REDCOAT III: You're just being neurotic.

REDCOAT II: *(angry)* What the hell do you mean – neurotic?

REDCOAT III: Don't be so touchy. I'm only saying *that (gesturing up towards speaker with her hand)* can only be effective in sleep. That's the whole principle of it, and that's why it's exactly timed to hit them in that very deep sleep.

REDCOAT II: I *know* that.

REDCOAT III: Well then, why . . .

REDCOAT IV: *(interrupting)* Actually, I had my doubts about it at first. I just wasn't convinced by the idea but, by God, it's been incredible.

HARRY: Did one of you check whether the loudspeakers in the are all working tonight? We have to be sure this is getting through to all of them.

REDCOAT I: Oh, for God's sake, Harry, we know our jobs.

HARRY: Why is this open? Who opened this window?

REDCOAT II: I did. Because it's too bloody hot in here.

HARRY: *(as if to close window)* There might be somebody out there.

REDCOAT II: *(sharp)* Leave it, Harry. Will you just leave it? We did the round. All the chalets have been checked. They're all asleep.

REDCOAT III: Why don't you just sit down and shut up. We've got work to do.

HARRY: There's no need to take that tone with me.

REDCOAT III: *(agreeably)* No? Oh, I think it's just the right tone to take with you, Harry.

HARRY: You wouldn't get very far without me, you know. How many of these people do you think would have come if I hadn't been here?

REDCOAT IV: *(bored)* Which is the reason you are here. The only reason.

HARRY: Well, as far as they're concerned, I'm the boss.

REDCOAT II: *(laughs)* You? The boss! You couldn't boss your way out of a self-addressed envelope. Do we have to waste time on your pathetic little ego?

REDCOAT I: Can't you get it through your head that they only brought you here because they wanted to use your name? You're just a can of beans on legs, mate, believe me.

REDCOAT IV: You're in no position to resent anything. If they hadn't brought you here, you'd be behind bars. They covered for you just in time.

REDCOAT II: Your finances wouldn't have made a very pretty picture for the fans, would they, Harry? All your little fiddles and fake companies.

HARRY: Alright, alright!

REDCOAT I: So. Sit down and shut up.

REDCOAT III: *(moderate exasperation)* Can we get on?

REDCOAT I: Right. The report has to be ready to go by morning. Here. *(Hands* HARRY *some papers.)* You can check these for date order. You can manage that, can you? *(*HARRY *sulkily takes papers.)* Now, has everybody seen all this?

Hands round folders, and they start looking through them in silence. Dim lights up on opposite downstage area.

TONY: Roger . . . wait. Where are you?

BOB: Shhhh! I'm over here. Keep your voice down.

TONY: *(moving towards him)* I don't get it. Why should Harry want to see me at four o'clock in the morning? Ouch! *(Trips and stumbles against* BOB.*)* What the . . . you're not . . . it's Bob! What are you up to? Why did you tell me you were Roger?

BOB: Because I had to get you here.

TONY: Let go of me!

BOB: Shut up. I'm not going to hurt you. Look! Look over there. Can you see?

TONY: Harry . . . and all the Redcoats. What are they doing? It's the middle of the night.

BOB: They're having a meeting. Betty wouldn't let me stay in the chalet . . . thanks to all of you. I've been wandering around for hours. I saw them going in there, so I followed them.

TONY: I'm going to tell them.

BOB: No, you're not. If you'd heard what I did, you wouldn't want to tell them anything. I came and got you because you have to hear this. You have to. Come on. There's a window open.

TONY: I'm not coming. Let go.

BOB: Tony, try to remember how you felt that night you told me you heard two of them talking. Think back.

TONY: That was all a mistake. I got it wrong.

BOB: No! You got it right. Just five minutes, Tony, okay? Just come and listen for five minutes and then you can do whatever you want . . . turn me in . . . whatever. I don't care.

TONY: *(unwilling)* Alright.

BOB: Come on.

They crawl over and crouch under window.

REDCOAT III: How many of this lot are going to be suitable material for Stage Two?

REDCOAT I: Probably about ten . . . maybe, twelve.

REDCOAT II: It's fascinating the amount of change – in a fortnight! Listen to this. *(Reads)* 'Subject Vera: on arrival, extremely reserved and quiet, pronounced stutter, physically awkward and timid in manner. By day Six, manifesting frequent but random aggressive outbursts. By day Ten, stutter non-existent, complete assurance of manner, hostility and violence level excellent. Clearly falls into leadership category.'

HARRY: *(bit defiant)* I took a lot of trouble with that girl.

REDCOAT III: *(not unkindly)* Alright, Harry. Nobody's saying you're not following instructions, but everything you do with them is on the conscious level, you see.

REDCOAT I: We operate on their subconscious area. That's where the real conversion work gets done.

REDCOAT III: Conversion's the wrong word. What we do is rearrange their personalities.

REDCOAT IV: Convert, rearrange . . . doesn't matter what you call it.

REDCOAT II: Don't be stupid, of course it matters. This *is* the pilot group, remember.

REDCOAT III: Absolutely. Every single thing we do with them – all our daily reports, our observations, the statistics tables . . . everything. It'll all go into the official Redcoat training programme. As far as I'm concerned, it's essential that all the terms we use are precise. Conversion isn't the right word.

REDCOAT IV: Okay, okay, I get you.

REDCOAT I: Let's leave the definitions 'til later, right? I'm a bit worried about the awareness factor. So far, we have no method of measuring how much they *realise* what they're doing.

REDCOAT III: Can't really be calculated . . . not with any accuracy.

REDCOAT IV: Yeah, right. All that kind of assessment is going to have to be done in Stage Two. In a laboratory situation, with special equipment.

REDCOAT I: Yes, that's true.

REDCOAT II: All we really know is when the violence component is triggered off, they go into an automatic emotional gear change. They *know* what they're doing but they don't have any sense of the rights or wrongs involved.

REDCOAT I: Which is exactly what we want.

REDCOAT III: Naturally. And all these reports show that after the violence episodes are over, they remember what's happened but they actually feel a sense of achievement and pleasure. Morality is obviously way down the priority list below ego satisfaction.

REDCOAT II: Well, that's not exactly a new idea, is it? If the history of so-called civilisation shows us anything it . . .

REDCOAT IV: *(interrupting)* Could we leave the theorising, for God's sake? We haven't got much time.

REDCOAT III: Point taken. Are we all agreed that piping the Sleep Teacher into the chalets every night has been successful?

REDCOAT I: Absolutely. It's brilliant.

REDCOAT IV: I don't know. Some of that stuff seems . . . I don't know . . . a bit melodramatic.

HARRY: Corny, you mean.

REDCOAT II: Thank you, Harry. How would we ever manage without your giant intellect.

REDCOAT III: I was on the team that researched the Sleep Teacher. All tests showed that subjects with a high aggression potential react very well to the heroic and poetic quality of those tapes.

REDCOAT I: Look at Hitler.

REDCOAT II: *And* Charles Manson. *And* Myra Hindley *and* Ian Brady.

REDCOAT III: There are any number of examples.

REDCOAT IV: Yeah. Okay. Got that. Does anybody think we have any borderline cases here?.

REDCOAT I: Subject Tony?

Noise outside.

HARRY: What's that?

REDCOAT II: What's what?

HARRY: I heard something.

REDCOAT IV: *(goes over, looks)* No. Nothing. Just sit down, Harry.

HARRY: I'm sure I heard something.

REDCOAT IV: So. Subject Tony. Yes?

REDCOAT I: His attitudes seem confused to me.

REDCOAT III: Not now. I had information from Subject Roger and I've kept Subject Tony under special observation. He's fairly stupid, but his loyalty is locked in now.

REDCOAT II: And he's got one of the highest hostility capacities in the whole group.

REDCOAT I: Right. Good report on Subject Rosie. There's a definite indication here that the over-sixties can be utilised.

REDCOAT III: Also Subject Freda. The semi-professional do-gooder. She's like a volcano inside.

REDCOAT II: *(laughs)* There's obviously a lot going for us in charity workers.

REDCOAT I: About tomorrow night. We've had our instructions.

REDCOAT II: Harry names the All-time Winners in the ballroom at twenty-three hundred hours, when the van will be waiting outside the gates for them.

REDCOAT IV: How do we know they'll all be willing to go?

REDCOAT III: Of course they will.

REDCOAT II: What? Receiving a special award on television? They'd go anywhere for that.

REDCOAT I: They couldn't resist it. The questionnaires showed us that every single one of them has always thought of themselves as superior. They'll go all right.

REDCOAT IV: Okay. That's it then, is it? Let's break up now.

All except HARRY *stand up.*

REDCOAT II: Come on, Harry. Beddy-byes.

HARRY *looks up and then gets up slowly.* REDCOAT IV *switches off the light in the conference area, leaving very dim light up on* TONY *and* BOB.

TONY: Have they gone?

BOB: Yes.

TONY: My God, Bob! It was like listening to devils. Nobody would believe it. They were right, though. I am stupid. I'm sorry, Bob.

BOB: Forget it. You've been conditioned, remember. Do you think you'll be able to break out of the conditioning?

TONY: After hearing all that? You bet I will. But why are they doing this? It's like some crazy nightmare. Who are they doing it for? What does it mean?

BOB: I don't know. I just don't know. *(Pause.)* But when you look around you, there're an awful lot of very violent things going on all over the world.

TONY: Yeah, but not planned like this . . . not like a chess game or something.

BOB: *(shrugs)* Who knows?

TONY: I feel like I'll never trust anybody again . . . never in my life.

BOB: *(after a brief pause)* Do you trust me?

TONY: Yes. You're different.

BOB: Thanks. *(Pause.)* What're we going to do?

TONY: I don't know. It's no use trying to warn the rest of them again. It just doesn't work.

BOB: Yeah.

TONY: But we've got to stop them on this Stage Two. God . . . laboratories! And I would have gone, Bob . . . I would 'All-time Winner' . . . oh yeah. It makes me sick to think of it.

BOB: So how can we stop them?

TONY: Tomorrow night . . . in the ballroom. We'll have to do something.

BOB: You mean, like a confrontation?

TONY: Yeah . . . yeah, that's right . . . a confrontation. I'll do it. I'll do it myself. A showdown.

BOB: I'll help you.

TONY: I can do it alone. I don't need any help. I'll trample those bastards like . . . like slugs. Like the filth that they are! *(He pauses, panting.* BOB *watches him.)*

BOB: I just wish we had a gun or something. Some kind of weapon.

TONY: I've got a flick-knife.

BOB: You do?

TONY: Yeah. Nobody knows about it. It's hidden in my chalet. I'm very good with a flick-knife. Fast.

BOB: *(again, after a brief pause)* You talking about killing someone?

TONY: What? *(Pause. Then slowly)* No . . . no . . . *(Pause.)* I'm just going to scare them. You wait. You'll see.

Blackout. ROGER*'s voice out of the darkness over the microphone. Very dramatic tone.*

ROGER: Out of the night that covers me
Black as the Pit from pole to pole,

I thank whatever Gods may be
For my unconquerable soul . . .
In the fell clutch of circumstance
I have not winced nor cried aloud,
Under the bludgeoning of chance
My head is bloody but unbowed.
It matters not how strait the gate,
How charged with punishment the scroll,
I am the master of my fate.
I am the captain of my soul.

Loud cheering and applause. Lights up on ballroom. Music. The campers milling about. ROGER *up on the platform with* HARRY. REDCOATS *standing at the side.*

HARRY: Wonderful, Roger, wonderful! Nobody could say our All-time Winners don't have all-time talent. Now, how many of our winners haven't performed in the talent parade yet?

CHARLES: Samantha. Samantha hasn't had a turn yet.

HARRY: Right, Samantha. You going to be our next star? Anybody else? *(Looks round.* TONY *is standing very still with his hand up.)* And Tony. Two more All-time Winners to go. Off we go, then. Ladies first.

CHARLES *leads* SAMANTHA *up the platform.*

SAMANTHA: Oh, honestly . . . I can't think of a thing to do.

HARRY: Anything, Samantha, anything you do is bound to be great.

JOE: Give us a little song, love.

SAMANTHA: Oh, all right. I'll sing a song. It's just a silly one. *(Sings)*
I wear my pink pyjamas in summer when it's hot.
I wear my flannel nightie in winter when it's not.
And sometimes in the springtime,

And sometimes in the Fall,
I climb right in between the sheets
With nothing on at all.

Cheers, applause, whistles.

HARRY: Oh saucy! Goodness me, Samantha, what would mummy say? Now, where's Tony?

TONY: *(immediately, he's standing behind the platform)* Here.

HARRY: *(jumps, startled)* Oh my God! *(Recovers himself.)* You gave me quite a turn. Up you get then, Tony. What's it going to be?

TONY: I'd like to tell a story.

HARRY: A naughty story?

TONY: No . . . more of a horror story, really.

BARBIE: Oh goodie! Is it really scarey?

TONY: Oh yes, it's really scarey.

ROSIE: I love horror stories. I love them, I love them!

DAVID: I've never been scared by one in my life.

TONY: You will be by this one, mate. *(Looks around generally.)*

REDCOAT I: Well, why don't you get started?

REDCOAT II: We're dying to hear it.

TONY: Alright. Once upon a time, there were four people sitting in a room one night, talking. Only they didn't know they'd left a window open. *(Pause. Looks at* HARRY, *then goes on.* HARRY *glances over at the* REDCOATS, *but they are all smiling.)* They didn't know someone was outside the window listening. *(His voice gradually gets louder, the words faster.)* They were talking about their victims . . .

some people they'd got hold of and were turning into monsters. They were talking about how they were going to send some of their victims off to a laboratory to be experimented on . . . to be changed some more. *(Very loud)* Stage Two, they called it. Stage Two!

HARRY: *(very fast and very hearty)* Well, that was a great story, Tony, terrific. Now, we'll . . .

REDCOAT IV: *(clipped)* Let him go on. He hasn't finished.

TONY: *(casual)* Oh, well, that's about it, really. Oh yeah . . . I forgot to say . . . the story's true. Oh, and another thing I forgot to say . . . *(With a very sudden movement he gets out his knife and flicks it open. Gets off platform and advances on the* REDCOATS. *His voice is very hard)* Four of the people were dressed in red, and the fifth one was called Harry.

DAVID: Oh, not that again.

JOE: Put that knife away, lad, a joke's a joke.

FREDA: I thought you'd got all those silly ideas out of your system.

SAMANTHA: Spoiling everything again, as usual.

VERA: He's just showing off. Stupid creep!

BARBIE: It's so boring! We're supposed to be having fun tonight.

They all ad lib *angry remarks to* TONY, *who turns on them, the knife out.*

TONY: Shut up!

They draw together and back away slightly.

HARRY: *(who has run over to the* REDCOATS*)* You have to stop him!

TONY: *(turning and taking a step towards* HARRY*)* You can't stop me.

REDCOAT IV: *(kindly)* No, of course not, Tony. Why should we?

REDCOAT III: Tell us some more.

REDCOAT II: It's fascinating.

REDCOAT I: Please go on.

HARRY: *(to* REDCOATS*)* Are you crazy?

TONY *takes another step towards them.* HARRY *scrambles behind the* REDCOATS *for protection. They just stand and look calmly at* TONY.

TONY: Tell them. You tell them. Tell them what I said was true.

REDCOAT II: *(pleasantly)* Of course it's true.

REDCOAT III: We're not denying anything, Tony.

HARRY: Oh my God, my God!

ROGER: *(puzzled, half-laughing)* What do you mean? What are you talking about?

ROSIE: I know what it is! It's a joke. They're having a joke on Tony.

JOE: What did I tell you, lad. You're making a fool of yourself.

HARRY: That's right, Rosie. You're right. It's a joke. Only a joke. *(Laughs a lot.)*

REDCOAT IV: Shut up, Harry. *(He does. Then to* CAMPERS*)* No, it's not a joke. Tony's right.

CHARLES: I don't believe it. We're not your victims.

REDCOAT I: You don't think so, Charles?

CHARLES: No, I don't! No! *(All* ad lib *indignant confusion.)*

BOB: *(moving to upstage centre)* Listen! I was with Tony last night. Outside that window. We did hear them. It is all true. They're using everybody here as guinea pigs.

BETTY: *(running to him)* Bob . . . I'm frightened.

BOB: *(puts his arm round her but talks to the others)* The ones who made the All-time Winners tonight are going to be shipped off to a laboratory. This camp is Stage One – that's Stage Two.

TONY: *(to* REDCOATS*)* That is true, isn't it? We heard you say it.

REDCOAT II: Certainly it's true.

REDCOAT III: That's right. Stage Two is for further treatment.

REDCOAT IV: The van's waiting outside the gates now.

REDCOAT I: All-time Winners . . . All-time guinea pigs.

The REDCOATS *laugh.*

VERA: They're laughing at us!

TONY: *(going over to* CAMPERS*)* You see? You see?

FREDA: Treatment? What treatment?

DAVID: What the hell do you mean . . . guinea pigs?

ROSIE: What have you been doing to us? Tell us.

REDCOAT IV: By all means, Rosie. It's very simple. We've been brainwashing you.

HARRY: Don't tell them. Don't!

REDCOAT II: You've all been conditioned since you came into this camp. Twenty-four hours a day.

REDCOAT I: The competition questionnaire showed that every one of you has a remarkably high violence potential. That's why you were selected. We've just been working on that potential, that's all.

REDCOAT IV: And it's been extremely successful. We're very pleased with you all. We really are. You're hardly human anymore. You're just machines for aggression. Sort of civilised savages, you might say.

HARRY: *(frantic)* Why are you doing this? You're mad. Can't you see they're dangerous?

Two of the REDCOATS *take hold of* HARRY *and push him out into the space between them and the* CAMPERS.

REDCOAT III: Harry's the boss, of course.

HARRY: No! No!

REDCOAT II: He's the chief.

REDCOAT IV: He's masterminded the whole operation.

HARRY: Don't listen to them!

REDCOAT I: He gave the orders. We just carried them out.

HARRY: It's a lie!

VERA: *(very savage)* Get him. Get Harry!

OTHERS: Yes! *(They start to move towards him.)*

HARRY: *(backing away)* Don't! Don't! Don't touch me! It wasn't me! They're lying to you!

CAMPERS: *(separately but overlapping each other, as they move to him)* Get him! Get him! Get him!

HARRY *runs upstage and gets behind* BOB *and* BETTY.

HARRY: Don't let them! For God's sake, save me. Tell them! Tell them!

BETTY: *(hysterically to* CAMPERS, *who are still moving)* Stop! What are you doing? You've all gone crazy. What are you going to do to him? What do you want to do? Do you want to kill him? Are you going to kill him? Is that it?

ROGER: Yes! Kill him!

Strobe light. Some of them grab HARRY *and throw him onto the floor downstage. The group converges on him at once, shouting. We hear* HARRY*'s screams as* TONY *stabs him again and again.*

BOB: *(over microphone, high-pitched noise underneath)* You have done well. You have remembered my words. Violence is victory. Violence is victory.

Absolute silence. Slowly, the group turns to face BOB, *who is up on the platform, his arms upraised.* BETTY *goes and stands in front of the* REDCOATS, *at the side of the stage.*

BOB: Your power is free.

Cut strobe light. A drum beat starts very softly, and during the following gets gradually louder and faster.

TONY: You! You were that voice . . . the . . . the Sleep Teacher.

BOB: *(gets off platform and joins* BETTY*)* Yes.

BETTY: We're in charge of this operation.

CHARLES: *(softly)* Oh my God, my God . . .

BETTY: *(laughs quietly)* Poor Harry. Poor, stupid Harry.

BOB: *(simply)* There had to be a sacrifice. *(To* CAMPERS.*)*

BETTY: Total. You've all become exactly what we wanted. *(She smiles.)* Vicious, unthinking pigs.

TONY: No! That isn't true. We're not vicious. We found out what was happening. We fought back. We're against you – we're not with you.

BOB: You're not *with* anyone. Violence is violence, and that's all you are now . . . that's what you've become. Violence can be turned against anyone . . . any time. You think you're a hero, Tony? We picked you because you had the knife. You did exactly what was expected of you. And you killed Harry . . . you all killed Harry.

BETTY: Killers – all of you. And you'll never be anything else. There's no going back now. You wanted to be winners? Well, this is the prize.

BOB: And now . . . move! The van's waiting for you outside. Move!

The group starts to shuffle forward in silence. The REDCOATS *cross over to them, two on each side of the group. There is a loud crash of drums as the curtain falls.*

On My Own Two Feet

Chris Hawes

Cast

KEVIN LEWIS

JEAN LEWIS

TERRY LEWIS

*DOROTHY

*DOCTOR

*1st SURGEON

*2nd SURGEON

*MIDWIFE

*CONSULTANT

*EDUCATIONAL PSYCHOLOGIST

*TEACHER

*TRACEY

*DARREN

*SALLY

*MR HIBBERT

*SOCIAL WORKERS

*1st DOCTOR

*2nd DOCTOR

*Two or more of these characters can be played, if necessary, by the same person.

ACT ONE

KEVIN's *wheelchair is seen in a spotlight. As the houselights darken, we hear the 'Blues for Kevin', played on a solo saxophone.* KEVIN *enters through the audience. He walks with great difficulty, twisting and jerking his body from side to side. At last, he gets to his wheelchair and sits down in it. The music fades and lights come up.* KEVIN *jerks about spastically. He speaks with difficulty.*

KEVIN: Hello . . . my name's . . . Kevin . . .

Gradually, his body straightens and relaxes. He speaks to the audience in a perfectly clear, normal voice.

KEVIN: Hello. My name's Kevin. Kevin Lewis. I'm what you'd call a spastic. That's why I walk like that, and talk like that. I have to walk like that and talk like that all the time. Except for now. Now I don't have to. I'll tell you why. I watch a lot of television – plays, films, stuff like that. I was watching a play one night, and I thought, 'I could do better than that'.

So I had a go. And this is it. What you're here for. My play. My life. I won't say any more about it. Except that . . . *(Kenny Everett voice)* It's all in the *best possible* taste. Right, then. *(Releases brakes on his chair.)* Chocks away, start t'play. First scene.

TERRY *and* JEAN *standing side by side, as in a photo.*

KEVIN: That's my dad. And that's my mum. Terry and Jean Lewis. I'm not in this bit. I'm not even born yet. Mum and Dad, they met at a disco. Went out for a bit, fell in love, you know what I mean. It does happen.

TERRY *and* JEAN *sit side by side, as in a car.*

TERRY: Jeanie . . .

JEAN: Yes, Terry?

TERRY: I think you're . . . Jeanie, I think you're really . . .

JEAN: You're the only one that calls me that, Terry.

TERRY: What, Jeanie?

JEAN: Yes, Jeanie, Terry. I like that. Everybody else calls me Jean. Dead boring, Jean.

TERRY: Jeanie, I . . .

JEAN: Yeah, what, Terry?

TERRY: I . . . er . . .

JEAN: By 'eck, you're a wiz with words, Terry, I'll give you that.

TERRY: No, I mean it, you see, I *do* . . .

JEAN: *(to audience)* Sat in that old banger of his, the Ford Escort, looking out over Lake Windermere in the Lakes. *(To* TERRY*)* Might even stop raining in a bit.

TERRY: Jeanie, you know, we've been going out for months now.

JEAN: A year. I counted.

TERRY: Well, and . . . love, you know . . . you know . . .

JEAN: I don't know unless you tell me, Terry. By 'eck, you're hard work sometimes.

TERRY: I . . . er . . .

JEAN: *(to audience)* I liked him because he was shy, not like them other lads – think they know all about it, God's gifts . . .

TERRY: Jeanie . . .

JEAN: D'you love me, Terry? Is that what you're trying to say?

TERRY: *(laughs)* Yeah.

JEAN: I think you're pretty amazing yourself. Is that it, or were there summat else?

Pause.

Let's get married, Terry? Is that what you were thinking?

TERRY: Yeah.

JEAN: Yeah, alright, then. Oooh, look! Sun's come out . . . lake looks nice.
Is that it, then?

TERRY: Is that what? D'you want a meat paste sarney?

JEAN: No, I don't want a meat paste sarney. I want a kiss. We've just got engaged.

TERRY: *(grins)* Yeah.

JEAN: So come here then, daft-head.

She kisses him. Blackout.

A loud burst of organ music: Mendelssohn's 'Wedding March'. In a spot, JEAN.

JEAN: It isn't like they tell you. In the love comics, once you've found Mr Right, once you've married him, all your troubles are over for ever and ever. In real life, they're only just starting.

Light up on TERRY, *seated, cleaning his saxophone.*

TERRY: I told you about the band. You knew about the band before we were wed.

JEAN: I didn't think I was marrying a band.

TERRY *tootles on his sax.*

JEAN: Go on, then. That's right. Play your saxophone. Fat lot of good it'll do you. That band'll never get anywhere. It's only a mucky old pub you play in, when it's there.

TERRY: Got to start somewhere, Jeanie. One day, you'll see, there'll be this big fat bloke in the audience – camel-hair coat, hat, big fat cigar – and he'll come up after the gig and he'll say, 'Any of you boys wanna make a record?'.

JEAN: Pigs might fly, Terry. You're a dreamer, you are.

TERRY: What's wrong with that? What's wrong with being a dreamer?

JEAN: I've got a dream. Getting out of this dump of a flat we live in – exist in more like – getting a house with a proper garden and enough room to swing a cat in, if we had a cat, which we don't cause there's no room to . . .

TERRY: I hate cats.

JEAN: Never mind cats. What about kids? I want to have a kiddie one day.

TERRY: Aye, but not yet, Jeanie. I mean, I love you, and *I* want a kiddie some day too, but not yet, eh? We can't afford a kiddie on what I earn.

JEAN: I love you too, Terry.

TERRY: Yeah, I know,

TERRY *plays a few bars of music, then gives up.*

I'm not in the mood any more.

Exit TERRY.

JEAN: *(to audience)* I get bored sitting at home every night. I'd like to have a kiddie. I sit and wait for Terry to come home. I cook his dinners, I stare at the telly. I'm bored. And I want a kiddie.

Blackout.

Light on KEVIN.

KEVIN: Did you ever hear the joke about the doctor and the

spazzo? Spazzo says to doctor, 'nngggn nyyanngg aaa' . . . Doctor says, 'Pardon?' . . . Spazzo goes, 'I *said*, "nnnggnnnaa nnagggaa nnngg"' . . . Doctor says, 'I can't understand a word you're . . .' . . . Spazzo goes . . . Hang on, here comes my dad . . .

Enter TERRY.

Finish the joke later. Back to the play.

Light on JEAN.

JEAN: Terry, love, I know it's going to be difficult . . .

TERRY: Difficult? *I'll* say it's going to be difficult. Are you sure, Jeanie?

JEAN: Course I am. The doctor said. *(Beat.)* I want to have it, an' all.

TERRY: Oh, yeah. It'll be great, won't it, bringing up a kiddie in this rabbit hutch. If you could only have waited a year or so. I'd be earning more money then. We could have got a bigger place.

JEAN: I'm not getting rid of it, Terry.

TERRY: Nobody's suggesting that, Jeanie. By 'eck! Fine thing, this is. Couldn't you have waited?

JEAN: Hang on a bit. What's all this 'you', 'you'? You had summat to do with it an' all, you know.

TERRY: *(arm round her)* I know I did.

JEAN: We love each other, don't we? We're supposed to be pleased about a baby.

TERRY: Yeah, you're right, Jeanie. Hey, tell you what. When he's a big lad, he'll be able to play in the band, with his dad.

JEAN: *(laughs)* What's all this 'he' stuff?

TERRY: Alright. If she's a lass she can be t'singer.

JEAN: You're hopeless, you are. I'll have to give up my job.

TERRY: Aye, but not yet, love. We need every penny coming in now. We're going to have to save for this baby.

JEAN: Yeah, I know. I'm worried, Terry. How're we going to manage?

TERRY: Oh, don't worry, Jeanie. We'll manage somehow. We'll survive.

JEAN *speaks to Kevin.* TERRY *stays.*

JEAN: I'm looking forward to you, Kevin. I can feel you growing inside me, from a little blob into a baby. I can even feel you moving. Then, later, kicking. Great, that feeling. Great. And being a mum-to-be's nice. Everybody like notices you. People give up their seats for you on the bus and that. People smile at you and wish you luck. You feel *important*. Terry's being ever so nice to me. He's looking forward to the baby too. We're both looking forward to you, Kevin.

KEVIN: I know, mum. I know you are. Only you don't know what's coming, do you? Nor do I. I'm quite normal at this stage – normal. Just like one of you. Warm, safe. Inside my mum.
(Beat.)
Have you heard the one about the three spazzos by the ice-cream van? They've only got enough money for one ice-cream, see? So, the first spazzo, who's an elegant speaker, says, 'We've . . . only got . . . enough money for one ice-cream . . . so the . . . one who can clap . . . his hands can . . . h . . . have it'. So the first spazzo goes . . . *(Tries to clap his hands, fails)* Second spazzo goes . . . *(Tries to clap his hands, fails)* Third one goes . . . *(Just about manages to clap his hands)* 'Great . . .', for it was he . . . 'I can have the ice-cream'. So they give him the ice-cream, right? Spazzo goes . . . *(Plunges ice-cream cone into*

middle of his forehead) 'Oh!'. *(Beat.)* Seven months later. Mum's getting really big with me now.

Enter JEAN. TERRY *reads his music paper.* JEAN, *very pregnant, spreads a blanket on the floor for herself and lies down on it.*

TERRY: What you doing, Jeanie?

JEAN: You *know* what I'm doing. I'm doing my breathing.

TERRY: Been down that ante-natal clinic again, have we? Teaching you to breathe now, are they? Very advanced.

JEAN: They're exercises, they're supposed to relax me. It's practice for when I have the baby. *(Doing them.)* Breathe *in* . . . one, two, three . . . *out* . . . one, two . . . *(Gives in.)* I've got to get it right, Terry, my appointment's tomorrow.

JEAN *tries to get the breathing right. Then gives in again.*

JEAN: Funny, going down that clinic. Takes ages for them to see me. I go in, I feel really *special.* You know, like *I'm* going to have a baby; like nobody's ever thought of doing that before . . . our baby, Terry's and mine. Open the door to the clinic, go in, there's dozens of other women, all pregnant like me . . .

TERRY: Amazing. You'd think that were what it were for.

JEAN: God, I feel heavy, I'm not sure all this breathing's helping. Ow! He *kicked* me, Terry!

TERRY: *(greatly excited)* Great stuff, Jeanie! A big strapping lad, you'll see.

Fade light on TERRY *and* JEAN.

Lights up on the ante-natal clinic. A strip light overhead. DOROTHY *comes in, very pregnant too, carrying a carrier bag. She rummages in it and pulls out knitting needles and a long unfinished scarf.*

KEVIN: My mum at the ante-natal. I make my presence felt.

DOROTHY: *(shouts across to* JEAN*)* Jean! Jean! How are you, lovey? All right, are you? Over here. *(Indicates chair next to her.)*

JEAN *sees her and comes to sit next to her, sitting with difficulty.*

JEAN: *(pain hitting)* Ooof!

DOROTHY: You're not due yet, are you?

JEAN: I don't think so.

DOCTOR *crosses the waiting room, in a hurry.*

DOROTHY: Here, doctor . . .

DOCTOR: Yes, Mrs Harris?

DOROTHY: It's Mrs Lewis, doctor.

DOCTOR: I'm sorry, I can only see you in order, Mrs Harris, you know that. Hang on, Mrs Lewis, I'll be with you as soon as I can.

He rushes off.

JEAN: I usually see that Indian doctor, Dr Patel.

DOROTHY: *(shouting after the doctor)* Charming! Never know who you're going to see!

JEAN: *(pain)* Oooh . . . it's not the doctors' fault.

DOROTHY: I know that. But it's somebody's fault, isn't it? I mean, look at us all? Crammed in here like cattle, we are. Battery hens, more like. Don't let 'em mess you about, Jean, that's my advice, straight.

JEAN: Yeah, right. Ooof!

DOROTHY: I think you might be about to have that baby.

JEAN: It can't be, though, can it?

DOROTHY: It can. It can happen. Happened to me with our Trevor. Terrible time I had with our Trevor.

JEAN: *(in great pain now)* I know, you told me that before.

DOROTHY: Oooh, I know, I get so bored in here I bore myself most of the time.

JEAN: *(screams)* Oooh!

DOROTHY: *(gets up and shouts in through the door)* Here! Doctor! Come here a minute.

DOCTOR *comes out.*

DOCTOR: Mrs Harris, I really must insist . . .

DOROTHY: Don't give me none of that malarkey, doctor. I think you'd better see to Mrs Lewis. *Now.*

DOCTOR: *(over to* JEAN*)* Mrs Lewis? Oh yes, I think you might be right, Mrs Harris.

DOROTHY *exits.*

All right, Mrs Lewis. Where are you feeling the pains? (JEAN *shows him.)* And are they regular?

JEAN: *Ow*. . . yes . . .

DOCTOR: I don't want to alarm you, Mrs Lewis, but I'm taking you in for observation. There is a possibility that your baby may be insisting on making his entrance a little earlier than anticipated.

JEAN: But I'm not ready . . . Terry doesn't know . . . I *can't* have him yet . . .

DOCTOR: There's no 'can't' about it, Mrs Lewis. We'll contact your husband and ask him to come in. What's his phone number at work?

JEAN: 634 . . . *oof* . . . 57.

DOCTOR: Yes, they are getting closer together now, aren't they? Now, look. I know this is all a bit alarming. But you really mustn't worry. Everything's in hand and perfectly normal.

JEAN: Normal? But I'm only eight months.

DOCTOR: Premature births happen all the time, Mrs Lewis. Perfectly normal, healthy, premature births. We're quite used to them, and we know how to deal with them. Don't *worry*, right?

JEAN: Yes, right, doctor.

DOCTOR: I'll leave you for a while now. Just relax and don't . . .

JEAN: Worry, no.

Exit DOCTOR. *Spot on* JEAN. *She talks to* KEVIN.

JEAN: Don't worry, that's a laugh. What does he expect me to do? I'm talking to *you*, Kevin. Daft, int it? But it's as if you're hearing me, listening to me. You aren't half giving me some hammer, Kevin. I've hardly ever been in hospital – only for that chicken pox when I were a kiddie. Then there were Mickey Mouses and Snoopys on the walls. No Mickey Mouses in this place. They're all whispering about me outside, I can hear them. Don't be so daft, Jean. Them doctors, they know what they're doing, they know what they're on about . . . I wish my Terry was here.
'Don't worry', that doctor said. Worries me to death when they say that.

Enter DOCTOR.

DOCTOR: Nothing to worry about, Mrs Lewis.

JEAN: Doctor, am I . . .?

DOCTOR: Are you what, Mrs Lewis?

JEAN: Never mind.

DOCTOR: Just relax.

He helps her to stand and leads her out.

Blackout.

Spot on KEVIN.

KEVIN: Sorry, mum. I didn't want to hurt you. I didn't want to come out of you. It's all warm and safe in there. Bed and breakfast. But you can't stop it, you know. It's life, birth, all of that. *(John Wayne voice)* 'When ya gotta go, ya gotta go . . .'. *(David Bellamy voice)* 'When the evolutionary pwocess first begins. When nature starts to take its course . . .'. I remember it. Well, not really – who can remember when they're born? But I dream about it. I dream about it all the time. It's not a dream, either. More of a bloody nightmare.

Blackout.

The stage is suddenly flooded red. Music: a slowed down version of 'Entrance of the Gladiators'. KEVIN, *in his dream, comes into the space and crouches down, watching. Through the audience, in a slow march, comes* TERRY, *dressed in a black morning coat, topper, carrying a cane.*

On the stage comes JEAN *in her white bridal gown. Red roses in her hair. Carrying her train, two white-coated* SURGEONS *with face-masks, white gloves, boots. Each wears a red pierrot ruffle round his neck.* JEAN *and* TERRY *move towards each other. She smiles at him, he smiles back. They join hands and together walk slowly up the aisle. The two* SURGEONS *fall over and pull off Jean's train, entangling themselves in it. Then the bridal couple return to the stage and pose for their wedding photo, with the* SURGEONS *as bridesmaids.*

TERRY: Cheese!

There is a flash. TERRY *addresses the audience, like a fairground barker.*

TERRY: And now! Ladies and gentlemen! For the first time! In the History of the Universe! The Birth! Of! Kevin! Lewis! and he's going to be *strong!*

ALL: Strong!

TERRY: And he's going to be *handsome!*

ALL: Handsome!

TERRY: And he's going to be *intelligent!*

ALL: Intelligent!

TERRY: But above and beyond anything else, ladies and gentlemen, he's going to be *normal!*

ALL: *Normal!*

KEVIN *curls up in a foetal position, ready for his birth. The two* SURGEONS *bring on a huge, blood-red paper hoop.* TERRY *joins* JEAN *and they pose for another photograph. The music builds. Suddenly,* KEVIN *throws himself through the red paper hoop. He is caught by the* SURGEONS, *who lower him to the ground. His body is deformed and twisted and he twitches there in a harsh spotlight. One by one,* TERRY, JEAN *and the two* SURGEONS *pull away from* KEVIN. *He is left helpless. Then a white-coated* ORDERLY *comes in with a wheelchair. He leaves* KEVIN *to struggle into it. When* KEVIN *has done so, the lights change to* KEVIN *as they were before this sequence.*

KEVIN: Nightmare.
Nightmare . . . joke about nightmares . . . right . . . *(Kenny Everett/Sid Snot voice)* 'evenin' fans. Sid Snot here. Had a nightmare last night. Been down the Dog and Whistle, see. Drank eighteen pints, puked up on the cat,

dreamed I was surrounded by these six skinheads and they was forcing a huge marshmallow down my throat. Woke up. Pillow'd gone.' Nightmare.
Wasn't a bundle of laughs for my mum, either. Right, normals. Next bit. I'm three days out of hospital.

MIDWIFE *on. She talks to an imaginary mum, and mimes the actions in this next speech.*

MIDWIFE: Hello, Mrs Robinson. Pop the baby on the scales. Oh, yes, very good. Everything all right, is it? Good.

JEAN *on, carrying the baby* KEVIN. *She holds him awkwardly.*

MIDWIFE: Hello, Mrs Lewis. Everything alright, is it?

JEAN: No, it's not. Everything isn't alright.

MIDWIFE: Why? What's the matter?

JEAN: He cries all funny. He goes all stiff when I pick him up. There's something wrong with him, nurse; summat not right.

MIDWIFE: I see. Is he eating well?

JEAN: I'm trying to breast feed, but he doesn't seem to want me. I'm ever so worried, nurse; we both are, me and my husband.

MIDWIFE: *(taking the baby from* JEAN*)* Alright, dear. *(Crosses to the window.)* We'll just take him over to the window.

JEAN: What d'you mean, over to the window?

MIDWIFE: *(at the window)* Haven't you noticed, dear? He doesn't like the light. Look, he's turning away.

JEAN: What d'you mean, he doesn't like the light? What are you saying? What are you trying to tell me? He doesn't like the light, what's that supposed to mean?

MIDWIFE: Mrs Lewis, I think we should get Kevin to a specialist.

JEAN: Specialist, what specialist? You don't think he's . . .

MIDWIFE: It's all purely routine, Mrs Lewis.

JEAN: *(very distressed)* What are you saying to me; what are you trying to tell me?

MIDWIFE: Don't get *upset*, Mrs Lewis.

JEAN: Upset, of course I'm upset! He turns away from the light, what's that supposed to mean?

MIDWIFE: Mrs Lewis. I want to make an appointment for you to see Mr Kramer. He's a consultant. He'll examine Kevin and make his report and then we'll know precisely what the problem is.

She takes KEVIN *out leaving* JOAN *alone.*

KEVIN: Mum and dad outside the consulting room.

TERRY *and* JEAN *sit on a bench.* TERRY *in work overalls. A striplight overhead.*

TERRY: Dunno why you had to drag me along here, Jeanie.

JEAN: I need you with me, Terry. I'm scared.

TERRY: There's no need to be scared. There's nowt wrong with him.

JEAN: He doesn't like the light, that woman said.

TERRY: He doesn't like the light! Course he doesn't like the light! He's *asleep* all the time.

JEAN: Terry . . .

TERRY: Stupid, these clinics. Don't know what they're on about half the time.

JEAN: Terry, *shush* . . .

TERRY: Don't shush me, Jeanie. Just don't do that, right?

JEAN: There's no need to get ratty.

TERRY: There's every need! I have to *work*, Jeanie, I should be *at* work, to earn money – for you, for me, for Kevin, for all of us. So what happens? Not only do you keep me awake half the night worrying cause he's so quiet (*quiet* for God's sake, not like most kiddies, screaming the place down) so not only do I get no sleep after a hard day at the factory, but you drag me in here to see some consultant and I lose half a day's pay. That's why I get ratty, Jeanie, that's why.

JEAN: I know it isn't easy, Terry. But you're not the only one.

TERRY: I *know*, love. I'm sorry, it's . . . getting me down all this, all this about Kevin . . .

JEAN: Kevin? *He* can't help anything.

TERRY: He's beautiful, love.

JEAN: I know that. But I think . . . I think I've always known it, and I haven't wanted to admit . . . Terry, it was that midwife in the clinic when she said, he doesn't like the light . . . *(Beat.)* It's like he doesn't want to *live*.

KEVIN: What the expert said.

CONSULTANT *in*.

CONSULTANT: Mr and Mrs Lewis. Cerebral palsy is caused by a lack of oxygen at birth. This lack of oxygen may lead to a greater (or lesser) amount of brain damage. Most children with cerebral palsy are born with perfectly well-developed muscles. The trouble is, they don't receive the proper signals from the brain, you see. This means that sufferers don't have proper control over their arms or legs. Nine times out of ten, intelligence, the power to think and reason, is quite normal, providing other parts of the brain haven't been damaged. Children with cerebral palsy are usually just as intelligent as anyone else. Some can do nothing physical for themselves. Others might have a relatively minor problem with walking, writing or speech. In short, no two cases are exactly the same. Because damage to the brain is never the same from one cerebral palsied person to another. Is that clear, Mr and Mrs Lewis?

TERRY: I've got a question. What is it that you're trying to tell us? Why don't you give it to us stright?

CONSULTANT: Alright, Mr Lewis. I will give it to you straight, if that's what you want. Your son is a spastic.

Pause. TERRY *stands up slowly and turns to the* CONSULTANT.

TERRY: *(softly at first, building to a shout)*
My son's not a spastic.
My son's *not* a spastic.
My boy *is not a spastic!*

Blackout.

ACT TWO

In blackout, the sound of applause, building. KEVIN *gets up from his wheelchair and walks forward to meet* TERRY *as loud rock music ('I want to be straight'– Ian Dury) belts out an introduction.* TERRY *tosses* KEVIN *a stage jacket.* KEVIN *puts it on.* TERRY*'s jacket is the same. As the song begins,* TERRY, *in mime, plays the sax part,* KEVIN *plays the bass.* TERRY *guides* KEVIN *through a step routine. Soon they are moving in unison.* TERRY *plays the sax solo,* KEVIN *backing him on bass. Then* KEVIN *grabs the mike and sings the vocal. Then something begins to go wrong.*

KEVIN*'s body begins to go out of control. He reaches out for* TERRY, *who pulls away from him.* TERRY *strips off his jacket and flings it away. He slumps down dejectedly.* KEVIN *stumbles to his wheelchair and sits in it. On the final word of the song: 'Straight', there is a blackout.*

Bring up a spot on KEVIN.

KEVIN: I'll never forget them looks my dad used to give me.
Always was a dreamer, me dad.
Right then, normals. I'm four now. In this scene, I'm upstairs being tested by an educational psychologist. Another expert.

TERRY *sitting, as at the end of the musical number. Enter* JEAN.

TERRY: Hasn't she finished yet?

JEAN: No, she hasn't.

TERRY: Take their time, these doctors.

JEAN: She isn't a doctor. She's an educational psychologist.

TERRY: Whatever she is, there'll be no improvement.

JEAN: What, in the doctor?

TERRY: Don't joke wi' me, Jeanie. I'm talking about Kevin. He's not going to get any better.

JEAN: He's *bright*, Terry. I can tell, I know he is. He can learn. He'll be a bit slower than the other kids, but he can catch up.

TERRY: Catch up? Our Kevin? Listen, I'm sorry to have to say this to you, Jeanie, but you don't know what you're on about. Bright? It's a joke. You only have to look at him. Where's he going to fetch up, then? Cambridge, I suppose.

JEAN: I'm not having him sent away, Terry.

TERRY: Yeah, you said. *(Moves to her.)* Look, Jeanie, I was talking to this bloke at work the other day, right? His sister had a kiddie who was spas . . . who was like Kevin, worse than him, and what they did, they got him into this special school. It's near Blackpool. He's getting on really great there, loving it.

JEAN: Terry, I'm not sending him away, and that's flat. I'm not! I'm *not!*

EDUCATIONAL PSYCHOLOGIST *hovers in the doorway, embarrassed at having stumbled in on a domestic row.*

JEAN: *(seeing her)* I'll go and make the tea.

Exit JEAN.

ED. PSYCHOLOGIST: He should be going off to sleep now.

TERRY: *(indicating* JEAN*)* I'm sorry about that.

ED. PSYCHOLOGIST: Oh, that's quite all right. *(She sits.)*

TERRY: Well? How did he get on, then?

ED. PSYCHOLOGIST: Very well.

TERRY: Oh? Brains, he gets from Jeanie. Looks, he gets from me.

ED. PSYCHOLOGIST: *(embarrassed laugh)* Ha ha, yes.

JEAN *comes in with the tea. She gives* ED. PSYCHOLOGIST *a cup, has one herself, ignoring* TERRY.

TERRY: What d'you think about this school business, then?

JEAN: I want him to go to an ordinary school, just like any other kiddie.

ED. PSYCHOLOGIST: I doubt if many ordinary schools are going to be prepared to take him, Mrs Lewis. That leaves us with the residential school, or the special day school, or the institution.

JEAN: He's not going in no institution.

TERRY: We've got to take the doctor's advice, Jeanie.

ED. PSYCHOLOGIST: It really depends on how well you feel you can cope with him here at home, Mrs Lewis.

TERRY: He's not going to get any better. We have to do everything for him, as it is. Or Jeanie does.

JEAN: That's right, Terry. *I* have to.

TERRY: You need a rest, love.

JEAN: Oh, you're so considerate, aren't you? It's Kevin I'm thinking about. He's going to have an education.

TERRY: Of course, I want that. *(Subsiding)* We just argue all the time with him here. *(To* ED. PSYCHOLOGIST*)* We might as well be honest.

JEAN: He's *not* going in no home!

Blackout. Light up immediately on ED. PSYCHOLOGIST, *reading from her report.*

ED. PSYCHOLOGIST: Kevin Lewis.

No need for intensive hospital care, though speech therapy and physiotherapy seem appropriate. His father says that Kevin is inclined to violent bursts of temper, while his mother tends to defend him and make light of problems, if she can. But even she admits that he is restless and not always cooperative.

The results of the intelligence tests aren't clear. He will be dependent on help in feeding and dressing.

The parents are not well off and lack formal education, and there seems to be some conflict as to what is best for Kevin.

I think it would be wrong for Kevin to be removed from his mother's care. I suggest placement in a special day school for the physically handicapped.

Enter JEAN *and* KEVIN. KEVIN *is in his chair, and* JEAN *is trying to feed him Redibrek. First she ties on a bib. Then she tries to spoon the stuff in. It's all very hurried and messy.*

JEAN: Come on, lovey. Here.

Enter TERRY.

TERRY: Why don't you let him feed himself, Jeanie? He's got to learn sometime.

JEAN: There isn't time. It's six o'clock. He's going to miss the special bus.

TERRY: Has he been to the toilet?

JEAN: He'll have to go when he gets to school.

TERRY: Wet himself on the bus, you mean.

JEAN: Oh, all *right!* I'll taken him in a minute!

KEVIN: I *could* feed myself, but it took ages.

Exit TERRY *and* JEAN.

She took me to the toilet, but I didn't always want to go. I mean, you don't *always* want to go, do you?

Right, normals. Next scene. On the loony bus. All aboard the loony bus, to the loony school! You sit on this bus, right, and the way it shakes you up and down makes you want to *go*, right? *(Peter O'Sullivan voice)* And good morning, ladies and gentlemen, and it's a fine morning for the Kevin Lewis Will-He-Wet-Himself stakes. And yes, Kevin Lewis is having his first outing of the week, so he's just a little bit *frisky*, but I must say looking at the runners and riders that he must surely be odds-on favourite this morning to wet himself before we get to the loony school . . .

And they're under conductor's orders now, and . . . yes, his bag is up and . . . they're *off!* And as they come down the High Street now, the going's good and bumpy, yes, and the driver is being very cooperative and driving all over the cats' eyes and Kevin Lewis is shaking up and down . . . And, yes, as we come down to the traffic lights in the High Street, I'm going to hand you over to Michael O'Hare for the rest of the commentary . . .

(Michael O'Hare voice) And thank you, Peter, yes, this is really very exciting as Kevin Lewis is thrown about from side to side by the motion of the loony bus, and I think I can see . . . yes, he's crossed his *legs* . . . yes, and the bus is really shaking now, and is he going to do it we ask ourselves; is he going to wet himself? And now, yes, he's crossed his eyes, fingers, arms and, yes, I think I can see them now looming up, yes, it's the gates of the loony school, and will he, won't he, yes, I think he *will* . . . I think as we draw up to the gates of the . . . *yes*, he's *done* it! . . . Great, great . . . Kevin Lewis has *wet* himself! *(Own voice)* I always used to arrive at that school in wet

Enter TEACHER. *He slots a tray onto the front of Kevin's wheelchair.*

TEACHER: Oh dear, Kevin, not again. What are we going to do with you? We haven't any clean clothes for you, you know. Alright, now then. Reading and writing. Kevin, pick up your pencil.

KEVIN *manages to pick up his pencil, then drops it again.*

Pick up your pencil, Kevin.

TEACHER *holds a card with 'CAT' on it.*

KEVIN: *(to the audience)* C, bloody A, bloody T, bloody CAT. I knew what the word was. I just couldn't get my hand to . . .

KEVIN *struggles to write.*

TEACHER: C, this is the C; A, this is the A, Kevin. T, this is the T. T, this is the T. C . . . A . . . T.

KEVIN: I know, I *know.*

KEVIN *breaks the pencil and throws it down.*

TEACHER: Temper, temper. Never mind, Kevin. We'll try again later. Here, play with these bricks for now. Put all the red bricks together and all the blue bricks together. All the blue ones and all the red ones, alright?

KEVIN: *(tries to get hold of bricks)* Stupid bloody bricks. Yes, I *can* tell red from blue. I'm not *stupid. I'm not bloody stupid!*

KEVIN *throws the bricks down.*

TEACHER: Oh dear, you are being difficult today. I know, Kevin, I do understand, you get frustrated, but you must keep on trying. Don't give in so easily.

KEVIN: That's easy for you to say, sweetheart. You haven't got a stupid body like mine.

Thing is, normals, if I played up, I knew I could sit in the sand-pit and he'd leave me alone for a bit, while he looked after the other kids. Some of them were worse than me.

TEACHER: Kevin, go and play in the sand-pit while I look after the other kids, would you?

KEVIN: Great! One up to Kev! No more stupid cat, no more stupid bricks. I get to play in the sandpit. In my wet pants. Next bit, normals. I'm nine now. We live in a council house. Nice. Got a garden an' all. I'm sitting in the garden right now.

TRACEY, *running.* DARREN *is heard off, chanting: 'One, two, three, four', etc., for hide-and-seek, cheating madly.*

TRACEY: Hello, Kevin.

KEVIN: Hello . . . Trace . . . *(To audience)* Tracey. Kid from up our street. She's my pal, is Trace. She's right nice.

TRACEY: Can I hide behind you, Kevin? I'm playing hiddy wi' Darren and he's it.

KEVIN: Darren, ugh! I *hated* Darren. *(To* TRACEY*)* . . . all . . . right . . . Trace. *(Aside)* Hide behind my chair any time, Trace.

TRACEY *doesn't understand at first. Then* KEVIN *swings his chair round and she gets it, and crawls into the space between the wheels. We still hear* DARREN *counting. Then he dashes in.*

DARREN Coming, Trace, ready or not.

KEVIN: *(aside)* I know where she is, Darren, you don't, *nyer*.

DARREN Can't understand *you*, Kevin. Trace! Where are you, Trace?

TRACEY *giggles.* DARREN *hears her and looks around.* TRACEY *giggles again.*

DARREN Hey, I get it. You're hiding behind Kevin, are you? Your pal, Kevin; our loony pal, Kevin.

TRACEY: Don't call him that, Darren.

DARREN Your stinky pal, Kevin.

TRACEY: Don't!

DARREN You should keep away from him. My mum says it's catching.

TRACEY: Your mum's stupid.

DARREN He's always stinky cause he keeps wetting himself. Here, want a sweetie, Kevin?

KEVIN: *(aside)* Not from you, sweetheart.

DARREN Go on, have a sweetie. Look, he can't even take it, he's stupid . . .

TRACEY: You're stupid, Darren Ellis.

DARREN Go on, Kevin, take one. They're mallows.

KEVIN: Ngggnnna . . . naggynnn . . .

DARREN Tell you what. I'll put it in your mouth for you. Your mam feeds you like this, don't she? Like a baby.

DARREN *rams the mallow into* KEVIN*'s mouth.*

DARREN Look at your pal, Trace. Look, he's slobbering.

TRACEY: Shut your face, Darren. He knows what you're saying.

DARREN No, he doesn't. He's a loony. Loony's don't understand nothing.

TRACEY: Shut up, Darren.

DARREN Don't you tell me . . .

TRACEY: I don't want to play with you *no more*.

DARREN You want to play with him, do you? You his girlfriend?

TRACEY: No, I'm not.

DARREN Girlfriend, girlfriend, loony Kevin's girlfriend!

KEVIN: *(aside)* She's not my girlfriend. I wish she was.

TRACEY: You just bugger off, Darren Ellis. I don't want to play with you *no more.*

DARREN *runs off, laughing.*

TRACEY: Don't take no notice, Kevin. *He*'s stupid. He pees *his* pants sometimes. I know, cause I sit next to him at school. I don't care what he says.
You alright, Kevin?

KEVIN: . . . Yeah . . .

TRACEY: I can sort of understand you. Well, I can't really, but I could learn to. I think it just takes you longer to say things than most people, that's all.

KEVIN: *(aside)* I want to *say* things to you, Tracey! I want to talk! I want to talk to you, using *words*, like the normals do! Tracey! *Tracey! Tracey!*

TRACEY: *(frightened)* I don't know what you're saying, Kevin.

KEVIN: *(aside)* I know you don't, I know you don't!

TRACEY: Mr Lewis . . .

KEVIN: *(twisting in his chair, getting more and more agitated)* Don't be frightened, Tracey . . .

TRACEY: *(shouts off)* Mr Lewis! Mr Lewis!

TERRY *runs in.*

TERRY: Yes, what is it, Tracey?

TRACEY: *(runs to* TERRY *and clings to him)* It's Kevin, Mr Lewis! I don't think he's very well!

KEVIN: *(his anger mounting)* I'm fine! I'm fine! I'm *not* having a fit! I'm not ill! I'm just trying to *tell* you something!

TERRY: He's having a fit! He's having a bleeding fit!

KEVIN: *I'm not having a fit!*

TERRY: Jean! Come out here!

JEAN *rushes on.*

JEAN: What's the matter? What is it?

TRACEY *rushes off crying.*

TERRY: Look at him! He's having a fit! I can't cope with no more of this, Jeanie.

JEAN: *You* can't cope! You can't cope! It's always 'you', 'you'! You don't think of nobody else!

TERRY: Well, you deal with it! *I* can't! I've had *enough!*

He stamps out. KEVIN *is very distressed.*

JEAN: *(goes to him, puts her arm round him)* It's alright, lovey. Everything's alright.

KEVIN: I wish I could talk to you, mum. I wish I could *tell* you. I only want to *talk* to Tracey like the normals do, using *words.*

JEAN: Can't tell what you're saying, lovey, calm down. Come on, I'll get you cleaned up.

She fetches a bowl and a flannel and begins to wipe his face for him.

There, that's better, isn't it?

Enter TERRY, *in outdoor coat.*

TERRY: I'm going out, Jeanie.

JEAN: Course you are, Terry. Band rehearsal, is it?

TERRY: Yeah.

JEAN: Well, you get along to it, Terry. Don't hang about here with me and Kevin. You'll make yourself late.

TERRY: Jeanie . . .

JEAN: Just go, Terry. *Go*! *(Finishes wiping* KEVIN'*s face)* There you are, my lovely boy.

KEVIN: *(aside)* I can wipe my own face, mum. Feels nice you doing it for me, though.

JEAN: I don't know what we're going to do about you, Kevin. Things are terrible between your dad and me. It's not your fault, lovey, but I don't know if I can cope any more.

TERRY: *(gently)* I think he should go in that residential school. They can look after him properly there.

KEVIN: I don't want to go to no residental school.

JEAN: It might be the best thing, lovey. We can give it a try, at least. If you're not happy there, we can bring you home again.

KEVIN: I won't be happy there.

JEAN: We'll come and visit you. And you can come home at weekends.

TERRY: *(warningly)* Jeanie . . .

JEAN: Well, perhaps not every weekend.

KEVIN: Alright, alright.
There's no point in arguing, normals. Nobody ever listens. I felt like *shouting* at the normals: Listen! Just because I can't talk like you doesn't mean I'm *stupid!* I can think as well as you . . . better than some.

The stage is flooded red. KEVIN *twitches in his chair. He hears voices of his persecutors, echoing.*

DARREN Loony Kevin, loony Kevin . . . loony school, loony bus . . . peed our pants on the loony bus, Kevin, aah . . .

TRACEY: Shut up, Darren Ellis.

DARREN: You his girlfriend, then?

TRACEY: No, I'm not.

KEVIN: I wish she was.

TEACHER: Oh dear, Kevin, what *are* we going to do with you?

KEVIN: Be my girlfriend, Trace.

TRACEY: Don't be silly, Kevin. How can I be your girlfriend? People like you don't have girlfriends.

KEVIN: Why shouldn't I have a girlfriend?

DARREN: Wouldn't you like to know, Kevin? *(Laughs.)*

JEAN: What are we going to do about you, Kevin? Things are terrible between your dad and me.

TERRY: I'm telling you, Jeanie. It's either him or me. Either *he* goes or . . . I mean it, Jeanie.

JEAN: I'm sorry, Kevin. But you see how it is.

KEVIN: Yeah, I see how it is. Go on, then. Shove me in that residential school. I don't blame you. Who wants to look at my ugly mug all the time? Sometimes I look in the mirror and I frighten myself.

Lights back to normal.

KEVIN: Right, normals. Residential school.
(Alan Whicker voice) And here we are at the Highfield Hall Residential School, wearing the old school tie, and the old school blazer. On my right, we have the amazing Sally. And on my left, we have the amazing Kevin. And yes, I do believe he's coming down the corridor now. Is it a plane? Is it a bird? Is it a flying piece of chalk? No, it's none other than Mr Hibbert, the secret mild-mannered identity of the Brain of Steel Superteach, and here he is coming into the classroom for the very first time . . .

Enter SALLY, *wearing leg irons.*

Enter MR HIBBERT, *carrying pencils and paper.*

HIBBERT: Good morning, everybody.

SALLY/KEVIN: Morning . . .

KEVIN: . . . Toi . . . let . . .

HIBBERT: Want to go to the toilet, do you? Well, alright. Off you go.

KEVIN: *(gestures)* Come . . . with . . .

HIBBERT: Oh, you want me to come with you? Well, alright.

MR HIBBERT *wheels* KEVIN *out.* SALLY, *left alone, grabs the box of pencils. She hides them. After a moment,* MR HIBBERT *wheels* KEVIN *back in.* KEVIN *is laughing.*

HIBBERT: You were having me on, weren't you?

KEVIN: . . . No . . .

HIBBERT: Then why couldn't you go?

SALLY: Too cold.

HIBBERT: I see. I've got a right pair here, I can tell. Alright, who's pinched the pencils? *(To* SALLY*)* Have you seen them?

SALLY: No.

HIBBERT: *(to* KEVIN*)* Do you know where they are?

KEVIN: . . . No . . .

MR HIBBERT *finds the pencils hidden under* SALLY'*s foot.*

HIBBERT: Tell you what, try and draw the tulip, Kevin. *(Puts tray on.)* There you go. *(Gives out paper and pencils.)* One for you, Sally. Is green all right? *(*SALLY *pulls a face.)* It'll do. *(He tips pencils onto* KEVIN'*s tray.)* Here are some pencils, Kevin, some coloured pencils. I want you to choose the proper colour for your flower. Choose the proper colour, Kevin. Red, the tulip was red.

KEVIN *chooses the red pencil.*

Try saying that, Kevin. 'The tulip was red'.

Blackout.

Lights up on TERRY *and* JEAN, *on a visit to the school, outdoor clothes on.* TERRY *carries the record, 'Ian Dury's Greatest Hits'.*

JEAN: Nice here. Clean.

TERRY: Jeanie, he's alright. They're looking after him great. He can feed himself now, they said. He can put his own clothes on.

JEAN: Oh, that's great, int it? Progress.

TERRY: It is for him, love.

JEAN: He's *clever*, Terry. I know he is.

TERRY: Now, come on, love. He's not clever. Accept it.

JEAN: He *is*.

Pause.

JEAN: It's so quiet at home without him.

TERRY: Yeah.

JEAN: I miss him, Terry.

TERRY: Yeah. So do I.

JEAN: I didn't think you did.

TERRY: He's my kiddie too, Jeanie.

JEAN: I thought you were ashamed of him. The way you'd look at him sometimes.

TERRY: Jeanie . . . I don't feel right proud . . . I didn't understand, that's all.

JEAN: Terry, let's have him home again.

TERRY: No, love. He's doing great here.

JEAN: It seems a good school. When we come I can really see him changing. Am I being selfish, Terry, wanting him home?

TERRY: Not selfish, love. Just not very practical, that's all.

Lights up on KEVIN. TERRY *and* JEAN *walk into his room and they all greet each other. They all speak at once.*

TERRY: Here you are, son. Bought you a record. 'Ian Dury's Greatest Hits'.

JEAN: How are you, lovey? You're looking well. Lovely to see you.

KEVIN: . . . All . . . right . . . *(Looks at record, to audience)* I've *got* it!

JEAN: *(leaving)* Tara then, lovey.

TERRY: Bye, son.

TERRY *and* JEAN *out.*

KEVIN: *(thinks for a moment, then)* Hey, Sally, want to buy a record?

Blackout.

Lights up on KEVIN *and* MR HIBBERT.*

*In performance, these 'teaching' scenes should be taken very slowly and deliberately. The aim is to show very clearly, and in as real a way as possible, the process of learning Kevin goes through, though of necessity in a very simplified form. The process is supposed to span years. The performers should use the text here as a guideline and find their own ways, through improvisation and their own research, of authenticating these scenes. (Author's note)

HIBBERT: Now, Kevin. I want you to do something for me. Look at me, and the shapes that my mouth makes, right?

KEVIN: . . . right . . .

HIBBERT: Say 'ah', Kevin.

KEVIN *struggles to say each of the sounds.*

HIBBERT: Now, try this one. 'Eh', Kevin . . . 'eh' . . .

KEVIN: . . . 'Eh' . . .

HIBBERT: 'Ee', Kevin . . . 'ee' . . .

KEVIN: . . . 'Ee' . . .

HIBBERT: 'Ooo' . . . you like this one, Kevin . . . 'ooo'.

KEVIN: . . . 'Ooo' . . .

HIBBERT: Now, 'aw' . . . you know, like John Wayne . . .

KEVIN: *(John Wayne voice)* . . . *Aw* . . .

HIBBERT: Good, Kevin, good.

Blackout. Lights up again on KEVIN *and* MR HIBBERT.

HIBBERT: Now, this time I want you to speak your name. Let's start with the K. K, k, k . . . come on, hit me with it, hard; right between the eyes, Kevin, scrambled egg, come on . . .

KEVIN: K . . .

HIBBERT: Now . . . ev . . . *ev*.

KEVIN: . . . ev . . . ev . . .

HIBBERT: In, Kev*in* . . . in.

KEVIN: . . . in . . .

HIBBERT: Now try putting it all together, to say your name, Kevin, K . . . ev . . . in. Kev . . . in. Kevin. Kevin.

KEVIN: *(really struggling)* Kev . . . kev . .

He gives up in frustration.

HIBBERT: *(getting up and walking away)* Alright, Kevin. If that's the way you want to play it. If you don't want to work.

KEVIN *makes a huge effort, and just as* MR HIBBERT *is about to leave the room he manages to say . . .*

KEVIN: Kevin!

HIBBERT: Great, Kevin. Well done! You've *done* it!

Blackout.

Lights up on HIBBERT, *holding a Zimmer walking frame and showing it to* KEVIN. *Some months have passed and* KEVIN'*s speech has improved.*

HIBBERT: Now, Kevin, you know what this is, don't you?

KEVIN: . . . A Zimmer . . .

HIBBERT: A Zimmer, that's right. Now, we're going to get some exercise today. Get up out of that chair. Come on, get up, Kevin.

KEVIN: Uh . . .?

HIBBERT: Come on, get up.

KEVIN *struggles to his feet.* HIBBERT *places a Zimmer frame around him.*

HIBBERT: Now. Take hold of the frame. There. It's alright. I'll I'll hold you.

KEVIN: . . . you'd . . . better.

HIBBERT: Now, Kevin, push the frame forward, then the left foot . . . then the right foot . . . that's right . . . get into a rhythm with it . . . frame, then left, great, then right . . . good . . . that's great, Kevin.

After several tries, KEVIN *begins to get the hang of it.*

HIBBERT: Okay, Kevin. Now I'm going to turn you round. Right?

KEVIN: Uh?

HIBBERT: *(turning him)* Let go of the frame, Kevin. It's all right, I've got you . . . now . . . get your balance . . . good . . . that's right. Now, I'll take away the frame – you don't need that any more, do you?

KEVIN: *(worried)* Uh?

HIBBERT: *(turning him)* Let go of the frame, Kevin. It's alright, I've got you. Now . . . get your balance . . . good, that's it, right. Now I'll take away the frame – you don't really need it any more, Kevin, do you, eh?

KEVIN: UH?

HIBBERT: No, you don't. Now, look. I've taken it away. Okay, so now I want you to walk back to your chair, right? Walk to your chair, Kevin?

KEVIN: UH?

HIBBERT: Go on, you can do it.

KEVIN *bravely and unsteadily stumbles the few paces to the wheelchair, in a titanic effort, finally getting there and flopping, exhausted into it.*

Blackout.

Lights up. KEVIN *in his chair,* MR HIBBERT *beside him.*

HIBBERT: Now, Kevin. We're going to do something a bit more restful today.

KEVIN: Thank . . . God . . . for . . . that.

HIBBERT: Now. D'you know what this is?

He brings out a unicorn attachment, which consists of a headband, and a probe which juts out from the wearer's forehead. At the tip of the probe there is a soft rubber.

KEVIN: . . . Uni . . . corn.

HIBBERT: And this, Kevin, is a communicator.

He brings out the communiator. This is a device, about the size of a large calculator, with letters of the alphabet and numbers on the keys. When messages are typed out, it extrudes a strip of paper, like tickertape.

KEVIN: C . . . om . . . municator.

HIBBERT: Now, you can type out messages on the communicator, Kevin. Just nod your head and touch the keys . . . that's right . . . like that . . . like that, Kevin, good. Now, let's see, what are you going to type?

KEVIN: 'Hello . . . dad . . .'

HIBBERT: Oh yes, he's coming to see you, isn't he? Well, go on then, Kevin, give it a try.

KEVIN *tries to type. He quickly gets the hang of it.*

HIBBERT: Now, come on, you don't spell dad with a 'z'.

KEVIN: Silly place to put a 'z'.

HIBBERT: I'll let you get on with it on your own, Kev . . .

He leaves KEVIN. TERRY *enters. He carries his saxophone. He stands watching* KEVIN *for a few moments, then moves to him.*

TERRY: Hello, son.

KEVIN *types.* TERRY *takes the piece of paper and reads it.*

TERRY: 'Hello, dad'. That's great, son. Well, Kevin. You're coming home, then. We're all going to be together again. The family.

KEVIN *types, 'Missed you.'.*

TERRY: *(reads)* 'Missed you.' Know how you feel, son. Well, you're sixteen now. Time to be standing on your own two feet, eh?

KEVIN *laughs.*

KEVIN: I can type now, on my comm . . . unicator . . . I can talk . . . much better . . . I can use the washing . . . machine . . . I can read and write . . . a bit . . . I'm . . . learning to . . . cook.

TERRY: Great, son. You'll be able to look after us.

KEVIN: Do you . . . like . . . toast?

TERRY: *(laughs)* Sorry I couldn't get down to see you last time. I've been playing with the band.

KEVIN: Are you . . . famous yet?

TERRY: No. Don't suppose we ever will be. That was just a dream.

KEVIN: It's all . . . right . . . having . . . dreams.

TERRY: I just like playing, that's all.

KEVIN: Dad . . . I can write . . . stories and poems on a typewriter. One day I'm going to write a . . . play . . . about all of us.

TERRY: That'll be a scream, I bet. Put summat in it about me, son. Give me a speech to say. I know how you feel, sat there in that wheelchair. You're trapped in a body that won't do what you tell it to. I'm trapped in summat else, always have been. Working in that factory, getting money, having a bit of fun now and again. In t'end, it all comes down to paying the bills and not letting the buggers grind you down. Thank God we love each other. We bloody need to.

KEVIN: Cheer . . . up . . . dad. You've got all that . . . toast to look forward to.

TERRY: I nearly forgot. I've written a tune for you. It's called 'Blues for Kevin'.

KEVIN: Take it away, baby.

TERRY *sits and plays for* KEVIN, *softly.* KEVIN *nods his head and smiles. Slow fade to black.*

ACT THREE

KEVIN *in his wheelchair. Warm light.*

KEVIN: Hello, normals. Back to normal now. Back at home now, in our council house, in the front garden soaking up the buttered bun. Haven't got a job, of course. But I've got a room of my own and a typewriter and a unicorn and I'm writing this play about us. Nice summer evening.

Enter TRACEY, *grown up now, pretty teenager.*

TRACEY: Hello, Kevin.

KEVIN: Girl from up the road, remember her? Grown up now. Hello . . . Trace.

TRACEY: Come over to say thanks, Kevin, for the birthday card. Did you do it yourself?

KEVIN: . . . Yeah.

TRACEY: It's really nice, Kevin.

KEVIN: Glad you . . . liked it.

TRACEY: Listen, Kevin. I'm going up the disco tonight. D'you want to come?

KEVIN: Me at a disco? Oh . . . yeah . . . that'd be a right . . . laugh.

TRACEY: No, it wouldn't, Kevin. It'd be alright.

KEVIN: I'd roll all . . . over the normals' . . . feet.

TRACEY: No, you wouldn't. Go on, why don't you come? I wish you would.

KEVIN: I'd be . . . embarrassed. Normals don't see . . . people like me . . . at discos.

TRACEY: Then it's about time they did.

KEVIN: They'd . . . laugh at me.

TRACEY: If they do, I'll beat 'em up for you.

KEVIN: *(laughs)* You wouldn' all . . . Why . . . d'you want to . . . ask me?

TRACEY: Why d'you think, Kevin?

KEVIN: Just sorry for me. Being . . . kind.

TRACEY: No, I'm not. I'm *not*, Kevin.

KEVIN: Poor little wheelie . . . kid . . . Shame, int it . . . aah! . . .

TRACEY: Yeah, right.

KEVIN: Like when I used . . . to . . . wee myself.

TRACEY: It's not true, Kevin. Right. I'll come round at eight. Right? Listen,Kevin, why shouldn't I ask you to come to a disco if I want to? Mmm?

KEVIN: . . . No . . . reason.

TRACEY: *(going)* Right, then. You're on.

Change to:
Loud disco music, and disco lighting, and DARREN *sauntering on, grown up now too, dressed in leather jacket, jeans, T-shirt. Then* TRACEY *enters, dressed in trendy disco style. She sees* DARREN *and tries to sneak past him without him seeing her. He sees her and she stops.*

DARREN: Hello, Trace.

TRACEY: *(cool)* Hello, Darren.

DARREN: You're looking good tonight.

TRACEY: Am I, Darren? Great. Glad you think so.

DARREN: You waiting for someone?

TRACEY: Yes, as a matter of fact, I am.

DARREN: And who's the lucky feller, then?

TRACEY: Wouldn't you like to know, Darren Ellis?

DARREN: Yeah, I would, cause if I *did* know, I'd . . .

TRACEY: Oh, would you? Well, watch yourself, cause here he comes now.

Enter KEVIN. *He's very trendily dressed and walking normally. He goes up to* DARREN, *who puts up one fist.* KEVIN *hangs his hat on it.* DARREN *slinks out. Then* KEVIN *and* TRACEY *dance, at first in the jerky style of punk dancing, then getting looser and more flowing and energetic. Then, something goes wrong.* KEVIN'*s movements become twitchy and constricted. He is seized by a fit. A strobe light flickers.* TRACEY *runs away from him, scared.* KEVIN *struggles down the ramp and into his wheelchair. The lights change back to the garden.*

KEVIN: Course, it didn't *really* happen like that. Tracey did take me to the disco in my wheelchair.

Disco lighting and music exactly as before. DARREN *enters, as before, then* TRACEY, *again seeing* DARREN *and trying to avoid him.*

DARREN: Hello, Trace.

TRACEY: Hello, Darren.

DARREN: You're looking good tonight.

TRACEY: Am I, Darren? Great. Glad you think so.

DARREN: You waiting for someone?

TRACEY: Yes, as a matter of fact, I am.

DARREN: And who's the lucky feller, then?

TRACEY: Wouldn't you like to know, Darren Ellis?

DARREN: Yeah, I would, cause if I *did* know, I'd tell him . . .

TRACEY: Oh, would you, now? Well, watch yourself, 'cos here he comes now.

KEVIN *wheeling himself in.* TRACEY *goes to him.*

DARREN: What? Him? What you brought him for, Tracey? It's stupid.

TRACEY: Why shouldn't I bring him?

DARREN: Ah, come on, Trace. What dance is he going to do, then, the locomotion?

TRACEY: Just bugger off, Darren Ellis.

DARREN *exits, mimicking the action of the spastic in* KEVIN*'s ice-cream joke, crashing the cornet onto his forehead.* TRACEY *moves to* KEVIN.

TRACEY: You're not having a very nice time, are you?

KEVIN: Very *kind* of you . . . to bring me. . . Trace. Very . . . *nice* . . .

TRACEY: There's no need to be like that.

KEVIN: There's every need! I don't want . . . charity . . . I don't . . . want pity . . . I want . . . I just want to be me, Trace . . . I just . . . want to be . . . *me*.

TRACEY: I'm sorry, alright? I made a mistake. God, you're really getting up my nose, Kevin, d'you know that?

KEVIN: I'm getting up *your* nose!

TRACEY: I try to do something nice for you, and . . .

KEVIN: Well, don't.

TRACEY: Alright, I won't. Look, you sent me that birthday card, Kevin, *that* was nice.

KEVIN: We . . . all make . . . mistakes.

TRACEY: Oh, charming. You can't be right all the time, can you? No, you're right. I didn't feel sorry for you, when I asked you out. *You* did. Just cause you're a spastic, doesn't mean I've *got* to like you, you know.

TRACEY *moves away from him.*

KEVIN: Aaah, normals. Our first little tiff, that. But important. Why? I think she *likes* me. I think she genuinely, really, actually *likes* me. Well, she did before I opened my . . . Tracey . . . I'm sorry.

TRACEY *turns and smiles at him.*

Blackout.

KEVIN: Back to normal, normals. Sat in our front room, staring at the telly. I like watching telly.

A knock at the door. SOCIAL WORKER *pokes his head round.*

SOCIAL WORKER: Hello? Anybody home?

KEVIN: Oh, God. It's old Supersnoop, the social worker, from the Social Services. I'll pretend to be asleep.

SOCIAL WORKER: Hello, Kevin. Asleep in front of the telly, I see.

He scribbles a note on his pad. KEVIN *deliberately 'wakes' with a cry and the* SOCIAL WORKER *drops his pad and pencil.*

SOCIAL WORKER: Ah, Kevin! You frightened me. Are your mum and dad in?

KEVIN: Mum's run off with . . . the milkman . . . and . . . dad's joined the foreign . . . legion. No, mum's popped out to the . . . shops and dad's at work.

SOCIAL WORKER: *(writing)* 'Both parents appear to have left Kevin on his own.' How are you Kevin?

KEVIN: All . . . right.

SOCIAL WORKER: Your speech doesn't seem to have improved much.

KEVIN: . . . no . . . nya nya nya nggnnn . . .

KEVIN *pretends to twitch and mumble, sharing a laugh with the audience.*

SOCIAL WORKER: *(writing)* 'I wonder if he may not be regressing a little, now he's at home.'

Enter JEAN, *carrying a full shopping bag. She sees the* SOCIAL WORKER.

JEAN: Oh. It's you, is it?

SOCIAL WORKER: Just popped in to see Kevin, Mrs Lewis.

JEAN: Kevin invited you, did he?

SOCIAL WORKER: No.

JEAN: You invited yourself. Again.

SOCIAL WORKER: I have to visit Kevin weekly, Mrs Lewis. You know that. Since Kevin left school he's become the responsibility of my department. He's on my caseload. Just doing my job, Mrs Lewis; just writing my report.

JEAN: Oh, yes? Hear that, Kevin? Be in the papers next. What's this 'regressing'? He's doing fine, he ain't regressing. *(She goes to* KEVIN, *kisses him.)* How are you, lovey? Alright? Watch some telly, did you?

KEVIN: . . . yeah.

SOCIAL WORKER: Watches a lot of telly, then, does he, Mrs Lewis?

JEAN: That's not all he does. I know what you're getting at.

SOCIAL WORKER: I have to make my recommendations . . .

Enter TERRY. *He stands listening.*

JEAN: I know your game. You're trying to get him put in a home. You're trying to make out we don't know how to look after him. He's happy here with us. You can write *that* in your bloody report.

KEVIN: You . . . tell him . . . mum.

SOCIAL WORKER: Mrs Lewis. Your attitude isn't very helpful.

JEAN: Helpful! I should think I'm not helpful. Your department isn't helpful.

TERRY: *(coming into the room)* You get my letter, then, Mr . . . er . . .?

SOCIAL WORKER: What letter's that, Mr Lewis?

TERRY: The letter I wrote to your department, asking if you could send someone round to help Jeanie out. Give her a day off from time to time.

SOCIAL WORKER: Mr Lewis, you know how it is – we're overstretched as it is . . .

TERRY: *(kissing* JEAN*)* Oh, aye . . . Hello, love. Hello, Kevin. Alright?

JEAN: He's round here snooping, Terry. He wants to put Kevin in a home.

SOCIAL WORKER: Mrs Lewis, I never said . . .

TERRY: No. Kevin stays here. That's definite.

SOCIAL WORKER: I have to make my *recommendations*, Mr Lewis . . .

TERRY: It's not up to us, then, what happens to Kevin?

SOCIAL WORKER: I didn't say that, Mr Lewis.

TERRY: Well, it is up to us. He's staying here. We're a family. We stick together. And I think you'd better sling your hook.

SOCIAL WORKER: Mr Lewis, I wonder if you've really thought about this. It's all very well, you say that you're a family, that you stick together. But Kevin will always be dependent on others for help in the ordinary tasks of life. Now, as long as you are alive, you can give that help. But what if you should meet with an accident, or your wife, or even both of you, God forbid? And what will become of Kevin when you eventually die? He'll have to become used to living in an institution at some time in his life. Wouldn't that be better now, when he's young and adaptable, than in later life, when he'll find things much more difficult?

JEAN: He's not going in no home, not if I can help.

SOCIAL WORKER: Over your dead body, eh, Mrs Lewis?

TERRY: Alright, I've heard enough. Now, you listen to me. We love Kevin. And we want him here with us, not just for his sake, but for ours, cause we *like* living together, all of us; and Kevin gives us just as much as we ever give to him – more, right?

Now, we might need some help from time to time, some money to put a lift in so's we don't have to hump Kevin up and down the stairs like a sack of potatoes. So's he can have a bit of dignity, for God's sake. Some money from your department to help Kevin live summat like a decent life and not sit in some home like a vegetable, cause you *become* a vegetable when they treat you like one, and we all know what them homes are like, don't we? It's not *your* fault, is it, Mr Social Snooper? Oh no, and it's not your department's, and it's not the council's, oh no, and it's not the Government's; oh no, not theirs – it's nobody's fault. Sorry about that, Kevin, old son, just your ruddy hard luck, int it?

Only, I tell you, Mister, I'm beginning to think it *is* someone's fault. It has to be, right? It *has* to be. And it certainly ain't mine. And it ain't Jeanie's. And God knows, it isn't Kevin's – poor bleeding Kevin's. Well, then. Who's fault is it, then? Eh? Think about that. Who's bleeding fault is it then, anyway?

Blackout.

Lights up on KEVIN, *as at the beginning of the play, in a spot, alone.*

KEVIN: Who's fault is it then, anyway? You heard my dad. I wonder about that. Why me? It could have been any one of you, you know. But it wasn't, was it? It was me.

Lights up on an operating table. 1st *and* 2nd DOCTOR *in white gowns and masks talk over* JEAN *as she gives birth to* KEVIN. *They have their backs to the audience.*

1st DOCTOR: He's not breathing. Oxygen.

2nd DOCTOR: God, the cylinder, it's empty!

1st DOCTOR: Get another one, quickly.

2nd DOCTOR *gets one.*

1st DOCTOR: I can't get the tube down his throat. Thank God. Turn the gas on now.

2nd DOCTOR: Is he going to be all right?

1st DOCTOR: He's breathing. We'd better get him to intensive care. There may be brain damage.

2nd DOCTOR: Mrs Lewis. It's a boy. You've got a little boy.

Fade light on DOCTORS.

Light up on KEVIN, *as before.*

KEVIN: That's it, normals. Tried to think of an ending, but I can't. What's the ending going to be for me? Or for the thousands of other people like me?
Tell you what, I'll finish that joke off. Spazzo and doctor, remember? Spazzo goes . . . *(mumble, mumble)*
Doctor says, 'I can't hear a word you're saying'. Spazzo

goes *(mumble, mumble, mumble)* Doctor says, 'Pardon? Spazzo goes *(mumble, mumble, mumble)* Doctor says . . .

KEVIN *loses the power of normal speech and reverts to mumbling and struggling to form words. He gets up from his chair and walks with great difficulty and slowness offstage, through the audience and out.*
We hear the sound of TERRY'*s saxophone playing 'Blues for Kevin', as at the opening of the play. And the play ends.*

Look-Sea

David Campton

Cast

RECITER

LECTURER

*HIM 1

*HIM 2

*HIM 3

*HER 1

*HER 2

*HER 3

MAYOR

COUNCILLOR LUGG

COUNCILLOR SOP

MAD SCIENTIST

MARINE BIOLOGIST

TANKER CAPTAIN

1st DELEGATE

2nd DELEGATE

3rd DELEGATE

*Him and Her parts can be played by any number of performers, and the lines shared between them.

When this play was originally broadcast it received the Minister of Education's award for the most outstanding programme for primary or secondary schools in the competition for the Japan prize.

On one side of the acting area is a rostrum for the RECITER. *This could have a reading stand or lectern if the poems are read rather than recited. On the other side of the acting area is a table for the* LECTURER. *This could have books, files or even scientific apparatus on it. Between the two is an area with blocks or low rostra.*

The RECITER *enters from one side and bows.*

RECITER: Thank you. Thank you. A recitation . . .

The LECTURER *bustles in from the other side with books, lecture notes, etc. Nods to the audience.*

LECTURER: Ah! Glad to see so many of you turned up for my lecture on . . . *(Consults notes.)*

RECITER: 'The Sea'.

LECTURER: I beg your pardon?

RECITER: *(with a flourish)* 'Roll on, thou deep and dark-blue ocean – roll . . .'.

LECTURER: *(interrupting drily but firmly)* 'The Ocean'.

RECITER: Eh?

LECTURER: *(reading)* 'The ocean, which although surrounding this earth, the home of the human race, with the ebb and flow of its tides, can neither be seized nor enclosed: nay, which rather possesses the earth than is by it possessed.' . . . Hugo Grotius wrote that three hundred years ago.

RECITER: I was about to say the same a minute ago. Now, if you don't mind . . .
'Roll on, thou deep and dark-blue ocean – roll!
Ten thousand fleets sweep over thee in vain;

Man marks the earth with ruin – his control
Stops with the shore . . .'

A group of HIMS *and* HERS, *dressed for the beach, run on to the acting area. They point to the sea and enjoy the feel of the sand between their toes.*

HIMS AND HERS: *(excitedly)* The sea! The sea! Look – sea! Race you down to it.

HER 1: Isn't the sea-shore lovely?

HIM 1: Hey! Mind where you put your feet.

HER 1: What did you say?

HIM 1: You nearly trod on a broken bottle.

HER 2: Yes, look. You might have cut a toe.

HIM 2: There ought to be a law against bottles on beaches.

HER 3: Look at the sea and sand. It's all so clean and fresh.

HIM 3: It might be if somebody cleaned away all the old cans.

HER 2: We're not looking for old cans.

HER 3: We're collecting seaweed.

HER 1: And shells.

HIM 1: There's a bit of seaweed.

HER 3: Where?

HIM 1: Sticking up out of the sand – brown and shiny.

HER 3: Oh, yes. Oh no, it isn't. It's a bit of an old boot.

HER 1: What's an old boot doing on the sea-shore?

HIM 2: The same as all those plastic boxes.

HER 2: They're chip boxes.

HIM 2: I know they're chip boxes, but what are they doing there?

HER 2: People throw them into the harbour when they've finished their chips.

HIM 1: Some people!

HER 1: Well, they've got to put their boxes somewhere, haven't they?

HER 3: Anyway, the tide washes them away.

HIM 3: The tide didn't wash these away.

HER 3: I expect it will next time.

HIM 1: And look at that. No, don't! I wish I hadn't looked myself.

HIM 2: Why do people have to turn the sea-shore into a dustbin?

HER 3: The sea's so big. Twice a day it comes in and washes the beach.

HIM 1: But what happens to the mess afterwards?

HER 3: Does it matter?

HER 1: When it's gone, it's gone.

HIM 1: Is it?

HER 2: Oh, don't bother about old chip boxes. Come into the sea.

With the exception of HIM 1 *they all begin to paddle.*

HIM 1: Wouldn't it be funny if somewhere in the middle of the ocean, there was a great pile of bottles and cans and plastic chip boxes, getting bigger and bigger.

Shrugs his shoulders and joins the others, paddling.

LECTURER: Funny? When Thor Heyerdal sailed his papyrus boat in the middle of the Atlantic, the sea around him was so filthy he couldn't put his toothbrush in it. You see, the water flowing past the coast of Africa carries with it all the rubbish that won't sink and that the fish won't eat. Several weeks later that lot turns up on the coast of America.

RECITER: *(casually)* Really? How interesting. I shall now continue with a little song about the sea. You can all join in the chorus, if you like. *(Starts to sing.)*
'Oh, I do like to be beside the seaside.
I do like to be beside the sea.'

HIMS *and* HERS *join in until the* LECTURER *interrupts.*

LECTURER: I say, I say, I say . . .

The singing dies down.

LECTURER: Do you really know what you like to be beside?

HER 1: The sea, of course.

LECTURER: Did you know that thirty-one seaside towns out of thirty-two discharge sewage into the sea?

RECITER: I don't wish to know that. A little song entitled . . .

LECTURER: And many don't even treat it first.

HIM 1: Hey, do you mean what I think you mean?

LECTURER: I mean the briny you're paddling in isn't all sea water. Some of it is flushings from the town's toilets.

HIMS *and* HERS *give cries of dismay.*

HER 2: Ugh! Untreated.

HIM 2: What do you mean by 'treated', anyway?

LECTURER: The sludge filtered and the dangerous germs made harmless.

HIM 3: You're telling us that, in some towns, they're actually tipping dangerous germs into the sea?

LECTURER: Where the sewage isn't treated.

HER 3: And we're paddling in it!

The HIMS *and* HERS *leave the water and go off, stepping very delicately, grumbling and muttering.*

HER 1: Somebody ought to do something about it.

LECTURER: What? How?

HIM 1: Well, if local councils are mucking up the sea, local councils ought to clean it up.

HIM 1 *and* HER 1 *go out after the others.*

LECTURER: You can always ask. But some things are easier said than done.

COUNCILLORS SOP *and* LUGG *enter arguing, followed by other town council members, each supporting their own side loudly. They are followed by the* MAYOR.

MAYOR: Please. Please. Everybody, please.

The noise dies down. Everybody sits, except the MAYOR.

MAYOR: This is a council meeting, not a supporters' outing. I am sure when Councillor Lugg spoke of dogs messing up their own doorstep . . .

COUNCILLOR SOP: There's no need to repeat it.

MAYOR: Councillor Lugg didn't mean anyone here in Slacksea.

He sits. COUNCILLOR LUGG *stands.*

COUNCILLOR LUGG: That's what you think. For years Slacksea has built up a reputation of being ideal for family holidays. How can we keep that reputation when our sea-shore is likely to send families to their doctors?

COUNCILLOR SOP: Nonsense. We're the chief tourist attraction on this coast.

COUNCILLOR LUGG: How many tourists are we going to attract when they learn what they're splashing about in?

COUNCILLOR SOP: They're not going to learn unless people like Councillor Lugg open their big mouths. We need tourists.

COUNCILLOR LUGG: We need a new sewerage system.

COUNCILLOR SOP: We need money for that. Where is it to come from?

COUNCILLOR LUGG: From the rates, of course.

COUNCILLOR SOP: So the rates go up and the hotel costs with them.

COUNCILLOR LUGG: I'm sure when tourists know how safe our sea is, they'll be glad to pay.

COUNCILLOR SOP: They won't, you know. They'll say Slacksea's too expensive and take themselves off to the Costa del Sol – sewage works or no sewage works.

COUNCILLOR LUGG: We are poisoning the sea.

COUNCILLOR SOP: I've lived in Slacksea all my life and I've not shown any sign of poisoning yet.

COUNCILLOR LUGG: Perhaps you don't bathe all that often.

COUNCILLOR SOP: We've tipped sewage into the sea for centuries. Why should we start paying for something we've always had for free? If the ocean isn't big enough to take our small contribution it's a jolly sight smaller than I've been told.

COUNCILLOR LUGG: I repeat – it's a dirty dog . . .

COUNCILLOR SOP *and all the other councillors speak angrily at the same time.*

MAYOR: This meeting is now closed.

The MAYOR *stamps out and the others follow, still arguing.*

RECITER: What a lot of fuss over nothing. As if Slacksea really mattered . . . *(Recites)*

'We watched the ocean and the sky together,
Under the roof of blue Italian weather.'

LECTURER: Italy? Who's going to Italy?

RECITER: Everybody's going this year.

LECTURER: But don't they know . . .?

HIMS *and* HERS *dash in with a beach ball, laughing and throwing it to each other.*

HIMS AND HERS: Who'll be first in? Come on. It's lovely and warm. *(Etc.)*

LECTURER: They ought to be warned . . . Excuse me.

The fun and games die down to a stop.

HIM 1: What?

HER 1: Who?

HIM 2: It's him again. The chap who tried to put us off Slacksea.

HER 2: Trust him. We're just having a quiet splash in the Med.

HER 3: And out he pops from under a striped umbrella.

HIM 3: Well, what is it this time?

LECTURER: I thought I ought to warn you that, of all the towns round the coasts hereabouts, only one treats its sewage before sending it out into the sea.

HER 1: You've got a one-sewer mind.

HER 2: Don't you ever think about anything except . . .

HIM 1: But we must have been swimming in . . .

LECTURER: You work it out.

HIM 2: Let's get out of here!

With a lot of squealing and shoving all the HIMS *and* HERS *go off except* HIM 3 *and* HER 3.

HER 3: The water looks so blue and beautiful.

LECTURER: You stick to looking at it.

HIM 3: Don't worry. As soon as we're dry, we'll have something to eat.

LECTURER: I hope you eat the right things.

HIM 3: Don't say it.

HER 3: You've stopped us swimming – you're not going to spoil our appetites.

They run out.

LECTURER: As if I would. I only hope they enjoy the food.

RECITER: Why shouldn't they?

LECTURER: Not just while they're eating it, but afterwards.

RECITER: Afterwards?

Chorus of groans off.

LECTURER: Afterwards.

HIMS *and* HERS, *wearing hospital garb, such as dressing gowns and/or pyjamas, enter groaning at every step. They sit.*

LECTURER: What was it?

HIM 1: I think it was something we ate.

LECTURER: Was it fish?

HER 1: Shellfish.

LECTURER: Ah! Shellfish.

HER 2: They looked lovely.

LECTURER: But you knew they'd been living in sewage-polluted water.

HIM 2: So what?

LECTURER: They were contaminated with intestinal bacteria.

HER 3: What are intestinal bacteria?

LECTURER: Germs that do you no good inside.

HIM 3: That's what we've got.

EVERYBODY: *(groans)*

LECTURER: If certain bacteria get into it, then the fish become unfit for human consumption.

HER 1: We know.

HER 2: We consumed it.

HER 3: Germs an' all.

EVERYBODY: *(groans)*

HIM 1: What germs, for instance?

LECTURER: Oh. Typhoid.

EVERYBODY: *(groans)*

LECTURER: Or hepatitis.

EVERYBODY: *(groans)*

LECTURER: Or cholera.

EVERYBODY: *(groans)*

LECTURER: Or dysentry.

EVERYBODY: *(groans)*

LECTURER: But in your case, you were lucky.

HIM 2: Lucky?

LECTURER: You'll survive.

HIM 2: Do you think so?

LECTURER: And at least you saw the Mediterranean while it was still alive.

RECITER: 'I must go down to the seas again,
To the lonely sea and the sky . . .'

LECTURER: It could be lonelier than you think. If nothing is done to stop pollution, by the year 2000 it will be quite dead.

HER 3: What do you mean by dead?

LECTURER: What do you mean? Killed.

HER 3: You can't kill a sea.

LECTURER: Everything in it can be killed. Imagine – no fish or seaweed. Not the slightest trace of life. It has already happened to some seas. It will happen to the Mediterranean unless the dumping of waste is stopped. Not just human waste, but industrial waste. You ate infected shellfish.

HER 1: Don't remind us!

EVERYBODY: *(groans)*

LECTURER: But at least it was there.

HIM 1: If it hadn't been, we shouldn't have eaten it.

EVERYBODY: *(groans)*

LECTURER: It could disappear altogether. The sea could die.

HER 2: So could we.

The HIMS *and* HERS *march out, groaning at every step.*

RECITER: Do you suppose I can get on now? *(Recites)*
'Tis said, fantastic ocean doth unfold
The likeness of whate'er on land is seen.'

He is interrupted by a peal of maniacal laughter off.

RECITER: Oh, not again!

Enter MAD SCIENTIST, *clutching a canister. He pauses to give a melodramatic laugh.*

RECITER: I beg your pardon?

MAD SCIENTIST: *(repeats the laugh)*

RECITER: Who do you think you are?

MAD SCIENTIST: I'm a mad scientist.

RECITER: Really? What are you doing here?

MAD SCIENTIST: I'm going to destroy the world.

RECITER: Good heavens, why?

MAD SCIENTIST: Because I'm a mad scientist.

RECITER: It takes all sorts to make a world.

MAD SCIENTIST: It's a mad scientist's job to destroy the world, isn't it? That's what we mad scientists are here for. *(Laughs.)*

RECITER: Well, how are you going to destroy it this time?

MAD SCIENTIST: Look at this.

RECITER: That tin of cocoa?

MAD SCIENTIST: It's not a tin of cocoa. This is a canister of deadly nerve gas.

RECITER: And what are you going to do with a canister of deadly nerve gas?

MAD SCIENTIST: I'm going to throw it into the sea.

RECITER: Ask a silly question . . . What happens then?

MAD SCIENTIST: It will rust through. And then . . . *(Laughs.)* I've bought some bombs, too. The Air Force lets me have them cheap when it's finished with them.

RECITER: Are they going into the sea, too?

MAD SCIENTIST: Where else? Then there are tanks of radioactive waste. The tides and currents will carry them to every corner of the world.

RECITER: So?

MAD SCIENTIST: The oceans will be destroyed beyond help – poisoned. And when the oceans have been destroyed, what will be left of the world?

He explodes into another peal of laughter, which is interrupted by the LECTURER.

LECTURER: Excuse me . . .

MAD SCIENTIST: What do you want?

LECTURER: I'm something of an expert.

MAD SCIENTIST: So what? You'll be exterminated with all the rest.

LECTURER: You're too late.

MAD SCIENTIST: Too late? I'm never stopped 'til the end of the story. We're only half-way through yet. What do you mean – too late?

LECTURER: When the United States decided to abandon nerve gas, it dumped its stocks into the middle of the Atlantic. In steel tanks.

MAD SCIENTIST: How dare they!

LECTURER: After the last war, the British Government got rid of its surplus bombs by slinging them into the sea.

MAD SCIENTIST: The fools!

LECTURER: And radioactive waste is already being piped directly into the sea.

MAD SCIENTIST: But the tides and currents will carry that all over the world.

LECTURER: Precisely.

MAD SCIENTIST: But that's dangerous. They could destroy the world.

LECTURER: Well?

MAD SCIENTIST: Help! They're trying to destroy the world. And I'm still on it. Help! Help! We're doomed. Help!

He rushes out, shouting.

LECTURER: Very unpredictable, these mad scientists. If I were you, I'd get on with your recital while there's still time.

RECITER: Thank you. *(Reciting)* 'Tis weary watching wave on wave . . .'.

LECTURER: Especially when each wave slaps another dab of oil onto the beach.

RECITER: Really!

LECTURER: Sorry. I was thinking aloud.

HIMS *and* HERS *run in, dressed for a day by the sea.*

HIMS AND HERS: The sea. The sea. Look – sea!

HER 1: Is that the Atlantic?

HIM 1: If this is Cornwall, that's the Atlantic.

HER 2: It's lovely. Nothing between us and America but sea and . . . Oh!

HIM 2: What's the matter?

HER 2: I've got black stuff all over my shoes.

HER 3: And me.

HER 1: Me, too.

HIM 3: Oil.

HER 2: Oh, no – it's more like tar.

HER 3: Sticky.

HIM 3: That's oil.

HER 1: It's a nuisance, whatever it is. These are new shoes.

HER 2: Half a mo'. I've got some tissues. Wipe the stuff off with them.

She hands out tissues and the HERS *sit down to clean their shoes.*

HER 3: It's like toffee.

HER 1: Yes. Sticks all over the place.

HIM 1: Don't look at me like that. It's not our fault.

HER 2: Trust you to bring us where there's oil.

HIM 2: There's oil all round the bottom of those rocks.

HER 3: What's it doing here, anyway?

HIM 3: The tide washed it up.

HER 1: The tide's supposed to wash muck away, not bring it in.

HER 3: I've got it all over my fingers. Give us another couple of tissues, will you?

HER 2: Sure.

She tries to get up, then stops.

HER 2: Oh – oh!

HIM 2: What's the matter?

HER 2: Anybody tried to get up lately?

The other HERS *try and meet with resistance.*

HER 1: We're stuck to the rocks.

HER 3: There must have been oil on them.

HER 2: Oh, why did we have to come here?

HIM 1: To see the sea.

HER 1: I don't care if we never see the sea again. Look at my shoes!

HER 3: My skirt!

HIM 3: Don't worry. It's only a bit of an accident.

HER 2: Do something about it.

HIM 1: Detergent. That's what we need.

HER 3: You can wash these rocks down at the same time.

HER 2: Yes. Give the whole shore a good wash.

LECTURER: Wait a minute. Are you sure you know what you're doing?

HIM 1: Sure. We're going to have a clean-up.

LECTURER: Have you heard of the 'Torrey Canyon'– the oil tanker that went aground on the Seven Stones, near here?

HIM 2: Of course we have; but what's that got to do with us?

LECTURER: An oil slick a hundred miles long stretched around our coast.

HER 1: I hope somebody washed that one off.

LECTURER: Oh, they did. The shore and rocks were sprayed with detergent. It took time and effort, but the beaches were cleared.

HER 2: That's what we need now.

LECTURER: The beaches were cleared of every living thing – seaweed, fish, worms, the lot.

HER 3: At least the beaches must have ended up clean.

LECTURER: Once the rocks were covered with mussels and limpets. Afterwards they were quite bare.

Enter angry BIOLOGIST.

BIOLOGIST: The pools were cleared of sea anemones. All killed. Not by the oil. By the detergent.

HER 1: We need some more here now.

HER 2: We're stuck.

BIOLOGIST: So whole populations of sea creatures are to be wiped out to keep your playground clean.

HER 3: What do you know about it, anyway?

BIOLOGIST: I ought to know. I'm a marine biologist.

HIM 3: Well, the mussels and limpets came back, didn't they?

BIOLOGIST: This time – yes. But it's going to happen again – as long as there are tankers. We live in the same world as the sea creatures. We can't afford to be selfish.

HER 3: Who's selfish?

BIOLOGIST: Oh, you wouldn't call it selfishness, would you? You'd call it convenience. Did you know that at the very time when everybody was cleaning the Cornish beaches, a tanker was discharging oil a few miles from the wreck? So convenient! What were a few more gallons of oil among so many!

Enter TANKER CAPTAIN, *truculently.*

CAPTAIN: You said it. If we are not spotted, who notices the difference?

BIOLOGIST: The birds that were brought into the rescue centre, black with oil. Those sticky bundles of feathers that were dying gulls.

CAPTAIN: I am sorry for the birds. But I am captain of a tanker. My business is oil.

HER 2: If oil is so important, why do you throw it into the sea?

CAPTAIN: We only throw away the waste. Impurities sink to the bottom of the tank. Very corrosive. The life of a tank is about twelve years. If cleaning stretches that life, it means money.

BIOLOGIST: So the sea is being polluted, just to make money for the oil companies.

CAPTAIN: You watch who you blame. You want oil and you want it cheap. Tankers have to be cleaned out. There is risk of explosion. Where do you want the danger – in port or at sea? I shan't say no more. You run your car on water.

He storms out, followed by the BIOLOGIST.

BIOLOGIST: That's not the only danger. What about synergy, eh? Have you thought about what happens when you mix . . .?

When they are both out, the RECITER *clears his throat.*

RECITER: May I now? *(Reciting)* 'What are the wild waves saying . . .?'

HER 1: Help!

HER 2: We're still stuck.

RECITER: I give up.

HIM 1: Why . . .

HIM 2: . . . doesn't . . .

HIM 3: . . . somebody . . .

HER 1: . . . do . . .

HER 2: . . . something . . .

HER 3: . . . about it?

LECTURER: There have been conferences . . .

Enter DELEGATES, *reading from papers.*

1st DELEGATE: We recommend a tightening up of discharge regulations.

2nd DELEGATE: We call for a pollution treaty to control dumping at sea.

3rd DELEGATE: We agree not to transfer pollution from one area to another.

HERS: That's nothing but talk.

The DELEGATES *raise and lower their arms as each tries to make a point.*

DELEGATES:

We propose . . .
We recommend . . .
We suggest . . .
We insist . . .
We decide . . .

HIMS: Talk. Talk. Talk.

ALL DELEGATES: We talk, talk, talk, talk . . .

They go out, flapping their arms like birds.

RECITER: Listen. Oh, you are listening. *(Reads)* 'The tremendous sea itself confounded me. As the high watery walls came rolling in, every fragment seemed possessed by the full might of its wrath. Masses of water shook the sea with a booming sound; the clouds fell thick and fast; I seemed to see a rending and upheaval of all . . .'.

He turns a page, but there is nothing on the other side. He shrugs his shoulders. He shuts his book and exits.

HER 1: It can't stop just like that, can it?

HIM 1: Can it?

LECTURER: Can't it?

He shrugs his shoulders and exits.

HERS: *(singing)* 'You may think that this is the end . . .'

HIMS: Well, it is.

Apple Blossom Afternoon

(Dave Sheasby)

Interview with the author

Where did the idea for the play come from?

I got the structure first: 'take an afternoon in a betting shop'. There's a time sequence – you enter and you come out. The idea of that structure interested me.

You can make a play about anything – but the problem is often the form. So I got the idea of the afternoon, and following one person through it, and one bet. The facts of that person's life didn't come 'til afterwards, nor did the gallery of other characters.

How do these characters 'come'?

As you start writing, I suppose. They do just come. And for this play I was spoiled for choice. Betting shops are strong on people.

The one in the play seems rather a sad place?

Sad? Not at all. Does the play suggest that? It's not at all sad.

The people in them are sad, then?

I don't think so. They're just a gathering of different people.

You go into betting shops yourself?

Yes.

In the play, Ted says his mum never understood why Billy goes in if he always loses and Ted says it's too difficult to explain. Can you explain why you go in them?

Because it's a bit of a habit. When you start doing something in a social, personal way, like going to the pub or smoking or going to church and going through the rituals – when you start into them, there's a sort of routine, a certain habitual thing. But habits can be enjoyable. And there's a lot beyond that – the atmosphere and excitement. And *money*.

For me, it's got a lot of excitement and passion and interest and involvement in it. I don't just stab pins into lists of horses, I read about them and follow them all the year and read books and have an interest in the trainers and jockeys and horses. I've spent a lot of time at it – since adolescence (I can't remember why I started). The interest's never died. I've often wondered why it doesn't get boring, but I've never been bored with it. It is also, for me, I say again, about trying to win money.

There may be some adolescents working on your play who'll get fascinated by it, like you were at their age, and go on doing it for ever. Would you approve of that?

There's no moral issue for me because I don't hold the view that betting is wrong. I can see why some people think it is and I am sure there are people whose lives have been spoiled by it. That said, for me it is not a matter of approving or disapproving. But for some people it's a real issue and I'm not dismissing that.

Which of the people in the betting shop in your play is you?

I'm a bit of all of them. There's all sorts mixed up in characters – including bits of yourself and false bits of yourself and fantasy bits of yourself. It's impossible to sort it out. That said, the one most *like* me is the student, Povey, who can't really make his mind up.

But there is a character in the play called 'Dave' like you, and he gets the best lines . . .?

'Back-pocket Dave'? . . . He hasn't got the best lines. He gets the winners, and he says some sharpish things about the racing world. But he's not me.

Do you know what happens to Ted after the end of the play?

No.

Don't you care what happens to him next?

I've never thought about it . . . He's only a creation. A fiction. I think I'll leave him there in the betting shop.

Do you think the play is in some ways a bit of a 'fix': the birthday, and a very recent bereavement and a big bet that comes up – with a photo finish – all in one day?

All plays are fixes. That's what 'art' is, says he pompously – a putting together of real life in the way you want it, for the purposes you want.

The photo finish is a bit of a 'fix', isn't it?

There are such things and they're terrible while you wait for the result. Especially if your bet depends on it.

But right at the end, when the whole bet stands or falls on it and thousands of pounds are at stake.

Yes – well, it is a bit dramatic, isn't it? (I don't want people to stop listening!) I think what your question implies is that it was a bit over the top for you. You prefer something more subtle. You may be right.

What advice would you give to students who want to perform your play?

They might go to a betting shop to see how it works, but there might be difficulties there because you have to be eighteen.

It's a prize-winning radio play – could it work as a stage play?

> Yes, I think so – it's in one little space. But the problem is the device of the narrator. You don't often get those in the theatre. It's regarded as being rather clumsy, but in radio it's a device you can use. And it would be a real problem because Ted's thoughts are central; they're what the play's about, rather than the betting. To miss that out would be to miss the whole point.

What novel, film, play, poem, song, etc., would you recommend to students working on your play?

> 'California Split', Robert Altman's film starring George Segal, all about two men who go on a horse and card gambling spree. They win lots of money, too. (So you see, it can happen!) But that's not the end of the story . . .

Advertising the play

'I don't want people to stop listening!' admits Dave Sheasby about his prize-winning radio play. But, first, people must *start* listening – in this case, by tuning in to Radio 4.

• Write 150 words for *Radio Times*, to try to persuade readers to tune in (e.g. '*Apple Blossom Afternoon* is the story of one man's . . .').

Reading the play

• In groups, with a spokesperson reporting back, discuss the play you've just read.

1 Do *you* feel it is a 'fix'? Would *you* rather have had an 'unhappy' ending? Or perhaps you don't think winning all that money is a 'happy ending', anyway?

2 This play was judged to be one of the six best radio plays of the many hundreds broadcast in 1988 – and won the prestigious Giles Cooper Award. Can you see why? Did it deserve to?

3 How 'sad' is the play?

Dave Sheasby says, 'I don't want people to stop listening'. Of all the plays, a radio play is the easiest to switch off. You're almost certainly already doing something else while you listen – and at any moment you can press a switch and get some other programme to distract you while you fix your bike, or feed the baby, or do your maths homework.

What clues can you get from this prize-winning play about how to keep people listening?

- Re-read the first few pages, making notes about how the listeners' interest has (hasn't) been 'grabbed'.

- Discuss in groups 'How to keep the audience switched on', using the evidence from this play – and any other tricks you can think of.

- Work out the opening five speeches of a radio play, guaranteed to keep the listener listening.

Rehearsing the play

The work that is done on a radio play in the recording studios is called 'rehearse/record'.

The work that follows is intended to help you with the coming task, which is to tape record *Apple Blossom Afternoon*. Local organisations might like to use your finished recording – as a 'talking book' for the visually handicapped for example.
The Royal National Institute for the Blind produces many of these 'books on tape'; it might be worth consulting them about copyright procedure before making your own recording.

Alternatively, you might choose simply to do a prepared reading of it – but to a real audience.

Radio plays are rehearsed differently from stage plays. *Apple Blossom Afternoon*, which lasted forty-four minutes and eleven seconds when it was broadcast, was rehearsed and recorded in the BBC studios in Manchester in only two eight-hour days. (A theatre play would be rehearsed for at least three weeks, and then be performed for perhaps another three.)

Some directors of radio plays work more like directors of films, recording in bits, in several 'takes', and not necessarily in the order of the script. Other radio directors do all the rehearsals and then record the whole play from beginning to end, in one 'performance'.

But very often, whatever the method, some of the actors never hear some of the scenes of the play they are in until it is broadcast. The director comes to the first morning of 'rehearse/record', with the play divided up into convenient units to rehearse and/or record. He/she will have asked the studio managers to gather whatever sound effects might be needed (on records and/or tape) and props for those which will be made during the actual recording. The actors (should) arrive having read the play several times and having worked out some idea of what their part is about, and how it might be read.

There is, of course, no learning of lines (the actors read from their scripts as they stand, or sit, at the microphones) though there are sometimes bits of 'scenery' in the different studio areas that create different atmospheres – doors that make door-shutting noises, pebbles that scrunch when walked on, a bed to lie down on if there is a bed scene to record, etc. There is no audience – except the studio managers at huge desks behind sound-proofed windows, mixing the sounds in the same way that record producers do. And possibly the writer, getting desperate. Rarely, plays are recorded 'on location'– which, in this case, would be in an actual betting shop.

- Discuss together at an early planning meeting, how you are going to tackle the job of rehearse/record for this play. You might need to appoint certain people to certain jobs at this stage.

- You are directing Dave Sheasby's play. Split the play into units that can be conveniently rehearsed/recorded separately. (It might help to do this work in pairs, and for each pair to take a few pages. The whole group can then agree to a complete list.)

For example, pages 1–4:

Unit 1 The tannoy announces the weather and latest news from Cheltenham in the early afternoon.
Unit 2 Ted narrates how things were at twenty-past four that same afternoon.
Unit 3 The tannoy commentates on a race at Cheltenham.
Unit 4 Ted narrates: what his mum used to say; what his boss thinks and what he thinks of his boss; the cats; and setting off to the betting shop earlier that morning.
Unit 5 Ted enters the shop and chats with Jane, who says he looks a bit 'washed out'.
Unit 6 Ted narrates: who Jane is and the untruth about Deirdre, etc.

The director (or an expert brought in from outside) explains how racing and betting work – via the sports pages of the newspapers. He/she demonstrates from one of today's races what all the numbers and names mean, and also explains with great care how an accumulator bet works. For example, in a £1, four-horse-win accumulator, you select a horse from four different races. All four have to win or you lose your £1.
If Horse One wins at, say, 2–1 you then have £3 (two times one, plus your own pound back) on Horse Two. If Horse Two wins at, say, 6–1 you then have £21 (six times three, plus your own £3 back) on Horse Three, and when that wins at 3–1 you have £84 on Horse Four. If that wins at, say, 5–1 you take home £504 (five times eighty-four, plus your own £84 back). But all four horses have to win or you lose the lot.

- Once you understand this, split into pairs. One person explains an accumulator to the other person, who is particularly dim and keeps asking difficult questions. Reverse roles.

'There's no moral issue for me because I don't hold the view that betting is wrong', says Dave Sheasby.

• In groups, discuss whether betting is wrong. What about the effects on families? Or on the person doing the gambling? Can you be religious and gamble? Is gambling a sign of immaturity? Of escapism? Would you care if your children took to betting? Would you let them read this play?

What changes would you make in the laws about betting? Would you let younger people go into betting shops? Or make it illegal to bet?

Looking at the characters

Ted

Dave Sheasby says that the 'gallery' of characters in the play came to him as he was writing it – and that betting shops are full of characters who could be in plays . . .

But it's Ted's play, really. It's the story of his winning afternoon – and it's his life and feelings about it that concern the writer and audience.

• Compile a 'dossier' on Ted. (Compiling a dossier on a character is a fairly common method actors employ to discover more about their characters. In a radio play, just as in a stage play, there are decisions actors have to take when interpreting how a character feels and talks if they are going to be convincing.)

• Read all of Ted's speeches:
(a) to other people;
(b) to himself.

• Work out a brief biography of Ted. Some of the questions will be answered or hinted at in the play; some you'll have to make up, but you should make them fit the Ted in the play. When was he born? Where? In what family circumstances? What about his father? What kind of schools did he go to? What was he good at in school? Girl friends? Was he popular? Childish hobbies? When did he start his interest in betting? Animal lover? What jobs has he had? Has he been married? Any children? Has he moved round the country? The world? Is he kind? Tolerant? Violent? Happy?

The 'hot seat' might help. (One or more people take the role of Ted. He answers questions about everything, whether connected to the play directly or not.)

• Make a list of people who remind you of Ted, or bits of Ted (from real life, television, films, books, poems, songs, etc.) and note what you think the similarities are.

For example,

1 My uncle – he studies horses and can remember races from years back.

2 Our neighbour – she lives on her own and . . . etc.

It might help to produce a time chart of his life (e.g. born Rotherham, South Yorks, only son of Marjorie and Stanley; aged 3, tonsils out; aged 5, All Saints Infant School – Miss Marden made him her pet because he was so quiet and hardworking; aged 7, first girlfriend, Janet, but she left him for Humpy Jones, who was good at football; etc.).

• In a radio play, the actors don't (usually) put on costumes to play the part. But listeners see more than a voice. Design Ted's costume. (How is he dressed, on his Apple Blossom Afternoon?)

• Twice Ted refers to 'loyalty', apparently contradicting himself (pages 30 and 32); discuss Ted's attitude to loyalty – and whether it is a key to the man he has become.

• If Ted had won his accumulator earlier in his life, things might have been very different . . . Tell the story of an earlier incident in Ted's life, which might have changed Ted's life, and show why it didn't.

• Dave Sheasby doesn't know what happens to Ted next. Do you?

The other characters

The other characters in the betting shop on this Apple Blossom Afternoon say, and do, less than Ted, but they still need to be acted and that involves more work than someone simply reading out the words into the microphone.

- Write a short biography of each of the following:

  Jane Dave Wesley Povey Billy

Go through the play for each in turn, noting what they say and do and what other people say about them. Make up the missing bits that you think are important.

Then, compare biographies.

- The 'tannoy', of course, isn't just a machine. There is a real person who eats, sleeps, drinks, thinks, etc., behind it, even though we only ever hear her (his?) voice. Explore different ways of playing her. Tell the story of the tannoy person, this Apple Blossom Afternoon.

- Good news! David Sheasby, the playwright, is coming in to rehearsal, just before you start your recording. Quickly (in quarter of an hour) list all the questions, doubts and concerns that you still have about the play.

- Bad news! Dave Sheasby has missed the bus. Provide your own answers to the questions and doubts and concerns on your list, and then –

- Record *Apple Blossom Afternoon* (and pass the tape on to be heard by other people).

After the radio is switched off

- Create a new radio play and record it.

- Take a character from *Apple Blossom Afternoon* and make a new play featuring this character. Or, take one of the other elements of Dave Shearsby's play as your starter (e.g. another story with a sporting or gambling theme, or another play about winning and losing).

The Winners *(Olwen Wymark)*

Interview with the author

Where did the idea of The Winners *come from?*

I'd been invited by the director, Lucy Parker, to do a devised play with the Old Vic Young People's Theatre Workshop. There were about twenty-five of them and it was a very talented group – in fact, five of them went on to become professional actors. The age range was seven to twenty, they all had terrific energy and amazing ideas and I got extremely fond of them. We did two pieces. One, *The Outsider*, was made up of scenes about lonely, eccentric or isolated people – a sort of montage; but for the other, we wanted a proper play, with a cast of characters and a good strong plot. The former was relatively easy; the kids improvised various characters and situations and I wrote some of them into scenes. The play was much harder and until we finally got going on it, I felt really hopeless and depressed. For one thing, though I'd done a devised play called *Find Me* the year before which went well, I still had doubts about devised plays – especially one with an invented plot. (*Find Me* was based on a real-life story.)

Where did the idea of the holiday-camp setting come in?

We talked and talked about possible places or situations which would accommodate a big cast – a boat, a religious community, a nuclear shelter after the bomb, but none of them seemed right. Then somebody thought of a holiday camp, but it wasn't until one girl said, 'Do we have to have a happy ending, Olwen?', and I said, 'No, don't let's', that I realised this holiday camp could be really sinister.

And what happened?

Lucy did a lot of improvising with them – innocent games turning savage, groups of quite ordinary people becoming violent, jolly camp activities becoming sinister and mysterious, and individual kids taking on characters and exploring the potential for hidden aggression. I taped a lot, took masses of notes and we had discussions. Then, in the three weeks that they rehearsed *The Outsider*, I went off and wrote the play. When I came back and read the play out loud to them, there was total silence when I finished. I thought, 'Oh God, they hate it'. But they suddenly burst out cheering and clapping and came up and hugged me . . . and off they went.

And off I went too, to work in New York, and didn't actually see it 'til its second run at the Young Vic.

How did it work?

I thought really well. They got a lot of laughs and they played with tremendous energy and concentration. It's quite a 'talky' play and they'd done excellent work on the text. Lucy had rehearsed them to a level of real precision. I felt, too, that this play utilised their natural bent towards what people call 'melodrama' but what I think is highly charged, passionate drama, and they really let rip . . . but in a disciplined way.

And what did the audience make of it?

We had an audience of all ages and I think they got the points we were making, and they were certainly attentive. A nine year old I spoke to said bluntly, 'I didn't like it'. 'You didn't enjoy it?', I asked. 'I didn't say that', he replied. Which was more or less the reaction we were after.

How did you 'find' the characters?

Mostly through the impros they'd done. Some I invented, to suit particular people in the group. The boy who played

Tony was called Tony and has since become a good playwright himself. We did a lot of work together on his character to make it unattractive *and* heroic. The boy who played Bob and The Voice had a very good vocal delivery and the girl who played Rosie was a natural born comic.

Are there echoes of sinister happenings from further away than an English holiday camp?

I hope so. I wanted a resonance of those American military camps where they actually teach torture, for one thing. And we did discuss the subject of all the vicious things going on in the world – South America, South Africa, Russian labour camps, the Ku Klux Klan, fanatical religious organisations – there was (and is) no shortage of examples. We talked about where the dictators, torturers, persecutors, etc., came from. Were they once just ordinary people? Also, I hoped we might strike a small blow against the greed and selfishness of our own acquisitive and self-centred society. And I'd seen a TV programme about an experiment in America. Ordinary people were asked to be guinea pigs and there was a victim (an actor) tied to a chair with electric wires attached, to whom they gave increasingly big doses of voltage as instructed by the presiding 'scientist'. Even when they could see that the 'victim' was in dreadful pain, they would increase the dose when the authority figure told them to. You could see they felt worried and anxious but most of them just did what they were told.

A critic of The Winners *said: 'It's a good menacing play but I'm not completely happy with the conclusion. The killing of Harry is made to appear essential but it depends on too many casual occurrences and why does this band of trained killers and leaders acquiesce so readily at the end.' What do you say to that?*

Well, the occurrences aren't supposed to be random – for

instance, the window of the hut is open deliberately and it is Bob who engineers Tony's experience. Also, the Redcoats orchestrate the murder of Harry by manipulating the group and its responses. We hoped that the shock relevation that one of the 'heroes' was the ringleader, the murder and the accumulation of the brainwashing would seem enough to reduce the campers to complete dehumanised robots, who would submit obediently to 'Stage Two' and become 'vicious, unthinking pigs'. The blood sacrifice is meant to be the turning point.

What advice would you have for a youth group staging the play?

Don't bother too much about sets. You need the bandstand and something ingenious for the hut, but the best effects are achieved by well-choreographed movement and good pacing. You have to maintain the tension in the scenes where there is a lot of talk or debate. I'd also recommend the kind of impro. work we did, and lots of discussion and even research and reading. I think the play should make us feel, 'This is about what's going on now'.

About what *that is going on now?*

About the terrible dangers of submitting to authority – elevating it above conscience and morality; about the potential in all of us for total self-centredness, betrayal of principle, repudiation of compassion, indifference to suffering – all that. Also, for me, the sort of generalised worry I have about any organised group in uniforms. If we had had a happy ending, *The Winners* would have been about the (genuine and undeniable, thank God) potential for good in human beings; this play is about cupidity, original sin and the evil that lives in us all.

Advertising the play

• You have twenty minutes to write a letter inviting someone you admire to come and see your forthcoming performance of *The Winners*. Explain that you have only just finished a first reading, but you can already say something about the kind of show it is, and what might be its appeal. Don't tell too much of the story.

Rehearsing the play

Olwen Wymark, the playwright who wrote *The Winners*, has come to your rehearsal.

• Make a list of a dozen questions you want her to answer, so that you can be clearer about what her play 'means'.

• Discuss your lists, and (possible) answers – in a full discussion in which your teacher is the neutral chairperson.

Casting the play

• Cast the play from amongst yourselves. Your discussions about who should be who ought to take into account the fact that sometimes it helps to 'cast *against* type – that is, not to go for the most immediately obvious casting (bullies aren't always big and strong; timid people don't always look timid, etc.). In other words, avoid stereotypes.

The best sight-readers are by no means necessarily the best actors – either in the National Theatre or in your group; it might help with your casting, therefore, to try an audition.

• In role, play out this audition for parts in a new production of Olwen Wymark's *The Winners*.

1 The director, casting director, associate director, and assistant director sit behind a table.

2 The people to audition come in, say who they are and which parts they are auditioning for, why they want these parts and why they think they would suit them.

3 The directors ask some questions.

4 They then ask each actor to 'give us your piece' – i.e. perform a speech by their chosen character from the play. This should be 'off the book' (i.e. known by heart). The actor is asked 'if there is anything else you would like to show us'. the actors may have something – another recitation, a speech by Shakespeare to read, a conjuring trick, a mime act, etc. – anything that will impress the directors to offer the part (for don't forget, in the theatre at any one time, eighty per cent of male actors and ninety per cent of female actors are out of work).

5 Sometimes at auditions, the persons being auditioned will be asked to do something surprising, e.g. 'Will you do your speech again, please, but at three times the speed?' 'Would you mind going to the back wall and shouting your part from there?' 'Will you read this in your Scottish accent, please?' Something surprising should be asked at these auditions of each actor . . .

6 Each actor is thanked and leaves. The directors discuss his or her suitability, and move on to the next person.

- Write a piece entitled 'The Audition'. (Do you sense any similarities between what might happen at an audition and what happened in the holiday camp?)

Looking at the characters

Each person should now be cast as a character in the play.

- Skim through the play, noting everything your character says and does, and everything other characters say about you.

• Try this actor's rehearsal exercise. (In the professional theatre, it is sometimes called 'actioning' the piece.) Talk through what your character does all the way through the play, e.g.

I am Harry. I ask if everyone's having fun. I say we're all winners and ask them to agree. I praise Rosie and her legs. I encourage everyone to dance. I make shy Vera jitterbug with me. I ask everyone if they are still having fun, and kiss and pat the day's winners as they are brought up to me . . . etc.

When the actors know their 'actions' right through the play, try fitting them together, starting at the beginning and going right through to the end, e.g.

VOICE: From the dark I encourage everyone to be tough and free and powerful.

HARRY: I speak into the microphone and ask if everyone's having fun.

ALL: We say we are.

HARRY: I say we're all winners and ask them to agree.

ROSIE: I agree.

HARRY: I praise Rosie and her legs.

ROSIE: I show my legs and dance.

ALL: We applaud and laugh.

HARRY: I encourage everyone to dance.

ALL: We dance, etc.

(This exercise in 'actioning' may take some time. But is an efficient way of finding out what a complicated play is really about. Misunderstandings will be thrown up, as well as disagreements about what is really happening under the words. By the end of the 'actioning', everyone knows the play very much better and some agreement should be beginning to emerge about what it 'means'.)

• Give your account of what happened to you at this strange holiday camp, in the form of a statement for the police. Work in pairs, as in an interviewing room; the 'accused'/witness tells the detective what happened; the detective writes it down; it gets signed. Then reverse roles.

Exploring the text

• Put together a five-minute version of the play. (You can either just improvise a quicker version, or go through the play choosing quotations, and then do the shorter version that you have created from the actual words the playwright wrote.)

• Olwen Wymark's story starts unexpectedly (in the dark) and goes on springing surprises. Go through the script listing 'turning points', where the audience suddenly realises things aren't quite what they thought.

• The playwright and director played 'innocent' games during rehearsals, and some of these appear in the play. Note all the games that are played in *The Winners.* How 'innocent' are they – even before they start 'turning savage'? What other children's games do you recall from playgrounds and cubs and brownies, etc? Did they 'turn savage', sometimes? There is a suggestion that children's games are a bit wild – and that the sort of bullying and manipulation that goes on in the camp is a bit similar to what happens in 'real life', in and out of schools? Do you think this is true?

Olwen Wymark, in her interview, talks about wanting a 'resonance' of other, real horrors from the world outside the theatre in her play – South Africa, etc. And she talks of the experiments with the electric chair. What 'resonances' do you feel from this play? Are there events in your own life you were reminded of? (Bullyings and scapegoatings?) Or things you've heard of, seen on television or read about? Other plays or stories you are reminded of?

• The playwright says that as they worked on making the play, 'We talked about where the dictators, torturers, persecutors came from'. Perhaps you could initiate a discussion along similar lines?

'I didn't like it.' 'You didn't enjoy it?' 'I didn't say that.' Olwen Wymark says that that was more or less the reaction she wanted. Untangle *your* reactions to the play. Do you find it depressing? Believable? Enjoyable? Chilling? What hope is there for human beings if they are so easily 'changed'? Are we perhaps all much nastier than we pretend?

The play doesn't have a happy ending. Many plays don't, of course, but you can still come out of the theatre feeling cheered and inspired, etc. But does this play offer any hope? Does it seem more or less likely that such horrors will happen?
Can you offer any hope, or advice, on how you might be able to let the audience go home having enjoyed themselves, in spite of the horrors? Or how the world itself might be made a bit more 'enjoyable'?

George Orwell's bleak novel, *Nineteen Eighty-four*, is at its darkest when the hero, Winston Smith, is 'brainwashed' into believing whatever he is told, and betraying his lover. Aldous Huxley's novel, *Brave New World*, deals with similar themes of controlling what people understand and know. They are by no means the only books dealing with the fragility of our individual selves when we are tortured or otherwise manipulated.

• With help from librarians and book lovers, and perhaps from organisations like Amnesty International, put together an anthology of material about brainwashers.

After the curtain comes down

The Arts Council have asked for your comments, in writing, on *The Winners*. Is it worth investing money in a new production? (You don't need to tell them the story – they already have a synopsis.)

On My Own Two Feet

(Chris Hawes)

Interview with the author

Where did the play start?

I was working as writer-in-residence with the Duke's Theatre-in-Education Company in Lancaster. A couple of years earlier, the company had devised and written a play about a boy with cerebral palsy, called *The Max Factor*, and there was talk about bringing it back – it had been terrifically successful in schools, opened a whole lot of people's eyes to what cerebral palsy's actually like (or rather it gave a rather limited but nonetheless genuine picture of what it is like) and what's more, it was very popular with local spastics who had seen it, which suggested that something important had been got right. We decided, instead of doing that play again, to write a completely new play about Kevin Lewis and his family, and to tailor it around the actors who were then in the company. For example, Dusty Hall, who played Kevin's dad, is a fine jazz musician and plays alto sax, so we changed the character's interest in football to an interest in music. And the lovely scene where Terry plays Kevin a blues came out of that. TIE companies usually work very much as cooperatives: through improvisation and 'devising' sessions in which everyone gets a chance to determine what the play is to be about and say, and the writer is in there to interpret those feelings and opinions, add his or her own and then make something consistent out of it. So many of the scenes in the play were roughed out by the actors and then written in more detail, and in what I hope is a consistent style, by me. Much of the monologue material that Kevin performs came from the ideas of Alan Turton, who played the character, and from a young cerebral palsied man called Vinnie, who came in to our rehearsals as a sort of adviser and stayed at Alan's house for a time.

How did you work on it?

Through contacts, like Vinnie, the local Spastics Society, a very remarkable woman who I met in Manchester, called June Maelzer, and through an organisation called PHAB, which brings able-bodied and disabled people together in a social setting, we tried to get things right. Alan Turton was able to get his movements more or less 'right' by working with Vinnie. It's terribly important that if anyone wants to do this play, they do their own research and find out for themselves the facts about the disease and not rely on the play to provide them. It's not a documentary. Of course, we read lots of books and articles and watched TV programmes, as well.

How did you discover the 'device' of Kevin's direct speech to the audience?

We wanted to get inside the character of Kevin, so that he could communicate with the audience directly, clearly, and without the usual barriers of speech that spastic people have to struggle with. We wanted to say, apart from his disease, Kevin is just as 'normal' as you are, but we also wanted to challenge the whole idea of 'normality' anyway. If the play's done well, very soon the characters who aren't spastic are seen by the audience very much through Kevin's eyes, and start to look most peculiar! 'Normality' all depends on where you're standing. The device works because audiences find it very releasing when Kevin starts to talk directly to them in their idea of a 'normal' way, and feel a sense of loss at the end when it's taken away. In real life, of course, it only takes a short time for a cerebral palsied person's speech to be quite intelligible to anyone who's prepared to have the patience to listen.

What difference does the play make?

When we asked spastic people what they hated most about the way they were treated by the 'normals' (their word, not mine) they were very clear about it:
– when they don't talk to us directly (the 'Does he take sugar?' syndrome);
– when they tell us how brave we are;
– when they patronise us;
– when they don't treat us as equally bright and capable, with an absolute right to all the privileges of a democratic country.

We tried to put those feelings across for a largely 'normal' audience. We were told by audience members that we had opened their eyes. Whether that has actually changed anyone's behaviour is, of course, another matter. Certainly, those of us who worked on the play had our attitudes changed.

You rather caricature the professionals?

I'm sorry to say that from our evidence and stories we were told, the picture we paint of insensitivity from doctors and social workers is, if anything, relatively generous to them. We heard the most terrifying stories. Of course, we all know that doctors and social workers are underpaid and overworked and there are some sterling examples of both to be found, but, honestly, it is difficult to find a cerebral palsy person who can find a good word for the medical or social work professions. Prove me wrong, but . . .

What reaction does the play get from spastics?

The spastics who came to see the play, and there were many, took it very much to their hearts. They felt the play was speaking for them, and it became 'their' play, after a while. But then, it was based on what they told us in the first place.

Whose 'fault' is it all?

The evidence seems to suggest that many cases of cerebral palsy come about because of brain damage at the moment of birth. Some of these have, in the past, come about through medical negligence. We don't have any statistics on this, but it is a significant proportion. The scene at the end of the play used to say, very definitely, 'medical negligence'. Now, I no longer believe that it's the only cause, and I'm on thin ice if I pretend that I have definite incontrovertible evidence. So, I'm hedging my bets here. The scene, as now written, leaves the question open. I don't know who's to blame. But, as Terry says right at the end, it has to be someone's bleeding fault, doesn't it? Let the reader decide.

What advice have you got for people interested in doing a new production?

If you want to mount a production of the play, research it. Find out. Meet some cerebral palsy people. Get to know them. This play, apart from anything else, and if it's done properly, arouses very strong emotions in people. You must be able to answer their questions or, at least, be able to point them in the direction of those answers.

Advertising the play

The director of the theatre has decided he will put on this play about a boy with cerebral palsy in the coming season. But you, and your colleagues in the marketing department of the theatre, are not too optimistic about audiences coming to see a play on such a subject.

- Discuss with colleagues the emergency publicity portfolio that will have to go out to make sure that audiences come in.
- Design a poster for the production.
- Write thirty words for a newspaper advertisement.
- Write 250 words for a press release.
- Draft a letter appealing for sponsorship, and draw up a list of possible sponsors (giving your reasons for supposing they may wish to put up money).
- Chris Hawes describes how *On My Own Two Feet* got put together. Write no more than a page explaining how the play was made (as a briefing document for any local radio interviews which you might be able to arrange to publicise it).

Reading the play

Chris Hawes says of audiences who have seen it, that this play 'opens their eyes'. Were your eyes opened by the play? Do you think your behaviour will have actually been changed by the play?

- In groups, discuss what you learned from the play – what surprised/disappointed/amused you; whose fault it was (if it was anybody's); what you are reminded of, etc.– and appoint a spokesperson to report back to the other groups.

Looking at the characters

Kevin

Try some exercises to experience some of the feelings of anger and frustration that Kevin sometimes has when he is not being treated properly.

• In pairs, try this rather difficult exercise that will require considerable concentration. One is a 'normal', one is a 'loony'. The 'loony', with no 'real' language or coordination, and *blindfolded*, must attempt to achieve a secret goal (e.g. the loony decides he wants the window open. He does not tell the 'normal'. The 'normal' is very keen to do what is asked and works hard to do it). It might help if you agree on a time limit, say, three minutes. Swap roles and try it with the 'loony' selecting another secret goal.

• Think through some childhood times, where there was always someone left out. Replay some of the games of the playground where some particular children are isolated or jeered at for the colour of their hair, or their glasses, or what they wear, or what religion or race they belong to . . .

• In pairs, tell of a time in your life when you felt you were isolated and victimised for being different.

• Write a story, poem, song, etc., suggested by this work. (You might call it 'Outside'.)

• Re-read all of Kevin's speeches – and discuss what kind of person he is.

The play itself is 'written' by Kevin – so, in a sense, the whole play is his speech. But he may have been untruthful in the play, or his perspective may have differed from that of other people, e.g. perhaps Darren is portrayed in such a hostile way because the 'author' (Kevin) is jealous of him?

• Discuss what sort of person Kevin makes himself out to be in his play?

• Compile a large list of adjectives that describe Kevin – that you can all agree on by brainstorming. (Dictionaries and thesauruses might help.) Here are some adjectives to start you off (you may agree on some, disagree on others):

Garrulous?	Optimistic?
Affectionate?	Unlovable?
Bitter?	Intelligent?
Witty?	Intelligible?
Selfish?	Self-absorbed?
Resigned?	Inadequate?

• Play a game of 'Scruples' with Kevin – i.e. think of as many *moral dilemmas* as you can, and work out together what Kevin's responses might be.

For example,

1 He finds a five-pound note in the street . . .
2 He is watching a favourite TV programme when a much-disliked neighbour pops in . . .
3 A gunman at the door will shoot his mother unless he stays in the way himself . . .
4 He is given too much change at the supermaket . . .
5 His handicap can be removed but only if someone living on the other side of the world gets it instead . . .
6 He is invited to come to church next Sunday and thank God for all things bright and beautiful.

• Using twelve quotations from 'Kevin's' play, show what sort of person he (thinks he) is.

• Do the research that Chris Hawes suggests in his interview. (Chris Hawes also recommends, as reading, Christy Brown's *My Left Foot*; the writings of Christopher Nolan, the prize-winning novelist who was freed to express himself through writing in the same way that Kevin is in his play; and Ian Dury's lyrics to his songs – especially, 'I want to be straight.').
There is also the Spastics Society, with pamphlets and literature– try the phone book for local branches.

• Discuss and display (and discuss the display) the fruits of this research, including material that seems to be connected less directly (photographs of the young and fit, for example; news of cut-backs in hospital provisions; new drug discoveries; other 'outsiders', etc.). Include in this display the songs or poems you write about Kevin, and all the Kevins, after reading this play.

On My Own Two Feet is obviously Kevin's play. But we also meet a number of the smaller characters in his life.

- Kevin has become a famous, published playwright, thanks to his efforts at his new machine. People who knew him when younger have been asked to contribute a shortish article (200–250 words) to the local paper on, 'The Kevin I Knew'. Contribute an article (writing as Darren, or Hibbert, etc.).

- 'Kevin Loves Tracey'. Does he? Replay the scenes between them.

- Write the song of Kevin and Tracey.

On My Own Two Feet is the story of Kevin, Terry, Jean, etc., from Kevin's point of view. We only ever know what he knows; we only have his words for what went on.

'His' story might look different through other people's eyes. For example, how did his parents *really* meet? (Kevin wasn't there, was he?) For example, what did they really feel when Kevin was due? And when he was discovered to be so severely disadvantaged? How did they cope? How nearly did their marriage break up? Did it, in fact, without Kevin knowing? What did the relatives say? Did his parents blame each other? Did they love each other? Do they now? Did they love Kevin? How important is Terry's music? What about the hidden and missing bits of Jean's life? What about more children?

Together, devise the play that tells the story of Terry and Jean – perhaps called 'Blues for Terry and Jean'. You might not have time to complete this assignment fully. You could shorten it by putting a time limit on the exercise below – by, for example, writing only a synopsis instead of the complete piece.

First, as the whole group, you'll need to agree on a time scale of events – when they met, at what age, how old they were when

Kevin was born, etc., and what other children there were (or weren't) etc. You will also have to decide what (if anything) happens next.

Then, working in smaller groups, take on responsibility for one part of the tale (e.g. between the birth of Kevin and his being sent away).

Decide how many scenes need to be written about this, and divide up the writing work. (You might find it helps to improvise and role play first, rather like the actors did in helping Chris Hawes write his play.) Both Terry and Jean can speak directly to the audience, but no one else can now (not even Kevin).

You might find it helps to write it as a serial, over several days – so that later episodes can take note of earlier ones.

Put the 'Blues for Terry and Jean' together.

Exploring the text

On My Own Two Feet isn't quite the documentary that it might at first appear to be – and that you might expect it to be, given the way it was built up. But it is a very 'theatrical' piece – things happen in ways in which they would not happen in real life (e.g. the birth scene).

- Go back to the script and break it into units.

- Then indicate against each unit how you would score its theatricality, scoring it out of ten. (Therefore, one out of ten would be the mark for a unit that was most 'naturalistic'– the closest to the way it would happen in 'real life.'

- Make a graph of the 'theatricality' of the play. On the vertical axis mark the scores 1–10, and horizontally, the units.

- Discuss what you learn about the play from this. Would you have preferred a more 'documentary' approach?

• Choose one of Kevin's monologues. Rearrange the sentences. Cut parts that don't seem to work (use a word processor if you can). What do you learn from this rearranging? Can you write better theatrical speeches than Chris Hawes, the playwright?

After the curtain is down

Simulation

There is the need for a home and some sheltered workshops for cerebral palsy victims, and other handicapped persons, in your immediate area. The land the council have selected to build it on is a children's playground, close to a very successful supermarket. The traffic on the road is bad and getting worse; the road could easily be widened at this spot. There is an infant school very close by. Many of the residents are old and easily frightened by change.

A public meeting is called to discuss what should happen. Among those present are:
The vicar (in the Chair)
The man from the council
A spokesperson for the elderly residents
A parent of a child with cerebral palsy
The Head of the infant school
A child who uses the playground every day
A doctor, who must be able to get in and out of his home for emergencies.
The manager of the supermarket.
A reporter from the local newspaper (who should write a newspaper report at the end of the meeting)
Others

• Role play this meeting. (Choose a character; prepare your case, and whatever documents and evidence you need; turn up at the meeting.)

Half way through the meeting, the news arrives that the Highways Department have decided that the road should now be one-way. A little later, the manager of the supermarket gets a message to say that his company could guarantee another fifty jobs if they are allowed to extend their present shop onto the children's playground area.

Towards the end of the discussion, a company of actors are invited in to perform Chris Hawes' play *On My Own Two Feet.* (You do not actually need to include this performance; but it might be interesting to read the play through again at this stage.) The actors are thanked and the discussion now continues. The vicar brings the meeting to a close by calling for a vote on what should be done next week.

Look – Sea *(David Campton)*

Interview with the author

Where did the idea for Look – Sea *come from?*

From a BBC producer – he's since gone off to write horror novels. He'd say things like, 'Go and write a twenty-minute programme on whale-hunting', and I'd rush to the library and get half a dozen tomes, take them home, and write. This time he said, ' I want something on sea pollution'. Now, at that time, I was teaching off the top of my head and producing a play a term in a college. Fortunately, the geography department there had just done a project on sea pollution and they gave me this massive file of press cuttings. I waded my way through all that.

I also had neighbours who were teachers (their daughter was just becoming a marine biologist) and they were in Cornwall at the time of the Torrey Canyon disaster. They were able to tell me such facts as, how the cure turned out to be worse than the original disaster. The rocks were cleaned – but everything else was killed.

How did you turn all this research into the play?

I decided I could only do it revue style. I needed short sharp sketches, linked in some way. That's why I had linking people – and started off with the lecterns to get over the more pedestrian bits.

The producer was quite fond of that passage in *David Copperfield* describing the storm. There was no way we could have got that in without somebody standing up and reading, 'The tremendous sea confounded', etc. So, in case anyone should ask, that extract is by Charles Dickens.

What about the humour in Look – Sea*?*

I find it very hard to keep humour out. It creeps in, almost unawares. The reciter and lecturer acts as comperes, but they are also almost stand up 'I-say-I-say' comedians, too.

And the other humour? The names of the councillors? Or the mad scientist, who starts out by telling us he is a mad scientist?

I listened to too many 'Goon Shows' on the radio in my misspent youth!

Why all the hims and hers?

Another thing I had in mind when I wrote the play was that it might be used with groups of young people. Classrooms and so on are a sort of amorphous mass where you may find you've got eight bodies or thirty. Like a caucus race, all must have parts. So the Hims and Hers are infinitely expandable or they could be reduced to one or two, if you're really hard up for actors.

How did you actually do the writing of Look – Sea*?*

I made lots of notes, then looked at the notes 'til people started to emerge from them.
For example, the town council scene came from reading a whole series of newspaper articles and minutes of councils 'til I could 'see' the people there. I've been on committees myself and seen how they work.

How long did the play take to write?

The writing was quite quick – the research took rather longer; a couple of months following up all the clues. But once the notes were in order, it happened in the speed of writing it down. I don't often write dialogue straight onto the typewriter, but I did with this.

What advice have you for people mounting a new production?

Keep the set as simple as possible. All you need are the two lecterns and a lot of imagination. People can have a lot of fun with props – things like beach umbrellas and lilos and things.

Let your imagination go.

Isn't the play a bit dated?

Perhaps in its examples.

I had to use the examples current at the time, such as the Torrey Canyon, and the Californian disaster that was even worse. But the situation is even more desperate now than when I wrote. I might have hoped that in several years something would have been done about it, but we've only talked and talked while the sea's got more and more polluted. If I were rewriting it now I might have brought in the seal problem in the North Sea. Or perhaps written about the North Sea rather than the Bristol Channel. Include the next outrage in the next production of the play!

If there's been no improvement in the pollution of our seas, plays like Look – Sea *don't seem to make much difference to the way the world behaves, do they?*

They might make some difference to the people who hear them or perform in them. Making some changes from the ground up? Let's hope that it does something for people with votes in their hands. Later on – it might be ten years, twenty even, before they have any impact – but that impact may come.

As with most seeds, you have to plant them, wait and see. On the continent – in Germany, in particular – the ecologists are already having an effect on the politicians.

Advertising the play

David Campton is not only a playwright. He is also a publisher of his own plays, which he advertises in various magazines, offering them to sale directly to theatre groups and clubs.

• Compose the 150-word advertisement for *Look – Sea* that would get amateur theatre groups, school drama clubs, townswomen's guilds, etc., hurrying to the post office to send for copies.
You might begin:
Play for sale! *Look – Sea* by David Campton.
Performance time – 15 mins.
Cast of fifteen, more or less.
A bargain, this play tells of . . . etc.

• In groups, find a better title – if you can.

Reading the play

How optimistic are you, after reading the play and what David Campton says about the way people's minds can get changed? Do you share the fears of some people who believe in a 'domesday scenario' – that is, the very worst will happen – and the sea will die?

• Contact the geography department, as David Campton did. See how much information you can find (as he did).

Ask friendly librarians for help with booklists, especially addresses of groups that will have further information. (See if 'Green' gets you anywhere in the phone books . . .) And while you're researching – what can you find out about the 'Torrey Canyon'.

• Research the 'Torrey Canyon', not from books or old newspapers, but by interviewing some older people (probably over thirty-five years old) who remember.

Take notes.

Then, compare notes. You might find that different people remember the same past differently. (You could find out about the 'Goon Show' this way, too . . .)

Exploring the text

The producer said, 'I want something on sea pollution'. So David Campton went and found out something . . .

• Make a list, in order of their appearance in the play, of the different sorts of sea pollution he found e.g. (1) p.152: broken bottles, an old boot, plastic chip boxes; (2) p.154: sewage.

• Look at your lists. Is there anything significant in the order the playwright chose?

Make a list, in order, of other writings about the sea he found from his research e.g. (1) p.151: Hugo Grotius; (2) p.153: Thor Heyerdal, 'Kon Tiki Expedition'.

Your two lists are the (perhaps) unlikely components from which David Campton made his play. The missing part, of course, is the playwright himself – yet that was the part that seemed to come most easily ('It happened in the speed of writing it down.') What did the playwright add?

At first read-through, *Look – Sea* might appear fairly simple. But when you start examining how it is put together, it gets more complicated. And odd.

Where is it *set*, for instance? There are scenes on beaches and in council chambers, etc., but everything's also happening in some sort of auditorium as well, where there is an audience. But what sort of audience? Have they come to see a play, or a poetry recital, or a lecture, or what? And who are these hims and hers who wander in and out, demonstrating various forms of sea pollution on various beaches that seem to appear and disappear between two lecterns? And what about the mad scientist who appears (on cue) to be mad and scientific?

• Divide the whole play into *units* (sections of the play that can conveniently be studied/rehearsed separately).
For example,

1 The reciter enters and prepares to recite.
2 The lecturer enters and interrupts. They tussle for the audience's attention.
3 Bathers enter 'the beach', spot litter, and go for a paddle.
4 One bather has a thought about a great pile of litter that might be in the middle of the sea.
5 The lecturer is reminded of what really happened to Thor Heyerdal.

• Now, discuss in groups, with a spokesperson to report back, 'this is a pretty weird play we're studying'.

Looking at the characters

The characters in *Look – Sea* aren't really 'characters', like those in the other plays in this book – and in most plays ever written. We don't find out much about them (even their names) apart from what they say, and what their occupations are. Some of them seem like cartoons. David Campton talks about the 'revue style' of the play.

But even if the writer doesn't mean his audience to be bothered about the things that concern the characters in more 'naturalistic' plays (who loves who? who can be trusted? who's dying? who's done the murder?), the actor still has to present something 'real' – and still needs to work with the director to discover it in rehearsal.

• You are going to direct the play. Make notes before the first rehearsal of what you will be looking for from each character. Jot down a list of your descriptions (five adjectives for each of the major characters). You might find a thesaurus or a dictionary of synonyms helpful (e.g. *reciter* – pompous, selfish, insensitive, irritable, foolish).

- Go down the list of characters and cast each part with someone you know – concentrating on how their looks and voices fit your descriptions above.

The penultimate stage direction in the play indicates that the reciter 'turns a page, but there is nothing on the other side'. What do you make of this 'image' (or physical picture)? Stage 'images' are often what people remember of plays long after they have seen them and forgotten all the words – as in, 'Oh, that was the play where at the end the person reading out the lovely descriptive stuff about the sea from Dickens suddenly found it wasn't there any more'.

- Devise three alternative 'images' to finish this play (e.g. the hims and hers come back on as mermaids and do a dying ballet, or brown, bubbling hot water rises and drowns everyone, or . . .).

After the curtain is down

The Domesday Trial of David Campton

It is Doomsday. David Campton, in his nightmare, is brought to judgement; accused of misleading the young. Among the panel of judges are:

1 *A Friend of the Earth*, deeply into protecting the environment and saving the world from all the many forms of destruction that threaten it. This Friend does not think the play is serious or up-to-date enough . . .
2 *A town councillor*, who is anxious to reject *any* criticisms the play might have about the safety of the seas, in case people stop taking seaside holidays . . .
3 *The Chairman of the Arts Council*, who likes old-fashioned plays with a beginning, a middle and an end. A strong story,

with strong characters preferably a 'whodunnit' . . .

4 *A teenager*, who can't understand what the play's on about but is very interested in pop music, football and videos . . .

5 *A businessperson*, who believes people have to have jobs, money has to be made, and profits, and if that means there is a litter problem, then somebody will have to sort that out . . .

The accused is: *David Campton*, a playwright . . .

On Doomsday morning, Mr Campton is brought before his judges and the case begins: 'Mr Campton, you are accused of the most serious offence of all – telling lies to the young. How do you plead, guilty or more guilty?'.

- In groups of six, role play his trial.

- Write up the Trial of David Campton (as a newspaper story; as a play; as a letter from the playwright; etc.)

'Include the next outrage in the next production of the play', is David Campton's advice.

- Do some research of your own. Using the geography department and the newspapers, find out about what's been going on in the seas since this play was written. Find five new facts about pollution. Do some research in poetry books and books of quotations for descriptions of how beautiful, etc., the sea is. Find five new quotations about the sea.

- Replace chunks of text from David Campton's play with your own new material on pollution and your own new quotations.

- Read/perform your new version to a live audience.

- Devise a short play about a different worrying aspect of the world we live in – cruelty to animals, say, or the ozone layer, or smoking, or . . .